STUDYING IN AUSTRALIA

STUDYING IN AUSTRALIA

A guide for international students

Teresa De Fazio

Routledge
Taylor & Francis Group

LONDON AND NEW YORK

First published 2008 by Allen & Unwin

Published 2020 by Routledge
2 Park Square, Milton Park, Abingdon, Oxon OX14 4RN
605 Third Avenue, New York, NY 10017

Routledge is an imprint of the Taylor & Francis Group, an informa business

A Cataloguing–in–Publication entry is available from
the National Library of Australia
www.trove.nla.gov.au

Illustrations by Kerrie Leishman
Set in 11/13 pt Adobe Garamond by Midland Typesetters, Australia

ISBN–13: 9781864488869 (pbk)

Dedicated to my teacher, my mother

Contents

Acknowledgments

I thank my family and friends for their unfailing support and patience. Special thanks go to my husband for his assistance; to my son for his inspiration; to Kim Borg for her creativity and good humour; also to Elaine Race and Pat Clancy for their helpful comments and encouragement. Particular thanks go to my students, who have shared their experiences and thoughts with me, and who never stopped asking questions. Final thanks go to Elizabeth Weiss and the team at Allen & Unwin for their guidance and confidence in the book.

Introduction

Embarking on tertiary studies is a different experience from any previous educational one. On first impression the institution is large, one's peers are unknown and the processes seem vague. It takes time to understand the expectations of lecturers and develop the necessary study skills to fulfil the requirements of tertiary education studies. This book provides insight into the expectations of lecturers and suggestions for developing personal study strategies through ideas I have gained in teaching for 15 years.

This book is designed to be a useful guide to TAFE students and to university students in the Australian context. It explores the tertiary culture peculiar to Australia, the services that institutions offer and cultural issues. This book aims to help make the adjustment process easier. It also provides practical advice on the preparation and presentation of assignments, the development of writing skills, the resources that are available, postgraduate study and time management skills. The book is meant as a guide that can be used throughout your studies to explain and enhance your understanding of important practical aspects of tertiary studies. Referring to certain sections or chapters will be as valuable as reading the whole book from cover to cover. This is why the book has been written so informally. Instead of another heavy academic text, you will find clear explanations, ideas on approaches to study and clarification of task requirements.

As you read, you will notice that the term *lecturer* is used to indicate anyone in a teaching position: a teacher, a professor, a tutor or a demonstrator. Also, the term *academic* is used in the broad sense to mean scholarly, educational or instructional, rather than referring only to a university environment.

The Australian tertiary education system

The Australian education system is divided into three stages: primary, secondary and tertiary. The first stage is primary or junior school (approximate ages 5–11 years), the second is high or secondary school (approximate ages 12–18 years). Tertiary education refers to the third stage of formal education, and is undertaken usually at a university, a technical and further education college (TAFE) or a private institution.

Traditionally, universities are academically oriented (with subjects such as literature, languages and medicine), while TAFE courses are more vocationally based (e.g. mechanics, carpentry and secretarial courses). This distinction is not quite so clear nowadays, with the introduction of new courses and course plans. However, generally, research oriented subjects are offered mainly by universities.

Tertiary education is centred around discussion, the sharing of knowledge, and the building of information and ideas around a specific area of study. Usually this area or discipline will lead to a student developing the sort of skills that will be useful in both a work situation and general life experience. Skills such as critical thinking, independent learning, researching, questioning and communicating are all important components of a repertoire required by modern life. The 'culture' or environment at tertiary level assists in providing the student with opportunities for relevant educational and personal growth. Courses at tertiary level are relatively specialised, with generally a vocational focus. Courses can be undertaken on site (some institutions also have different campuses including overseas-based campuses) or by distance learning.

LEARNING ACTIVITIES AND THE ACADEMIC CALENDAR

Tertiary study life is taken up with learning, research and discussion. You will experience various types of learning environments—lectures, tutorials, workshops, seminars, laboratory sessions, practicums and so on. You will undertake research using information from different sources, such as course material, library texts and online data, and gain a lot of helpful information from discussion in both structured and informal settings.

There are a number of ways in which you will be expected to demonstrate what you have learnt, through:

- tutorial participation
- essay writing
- reports
- thesis/dissertation
- research projects
- case studies
- oral presentations
- examinations
- literature review
- reports.

The scholastic year varies, depending on the institution. The TAFE year runs from February to December. University courses usually run for two semesters, beginning late February or early March, and finish late November (this includes examination time). Some institutions are now offering a trimester system (three semesters) and summer schools. Courses at private training colleges normally run all year, with a short break from the end of December to early January for Christmas. Check with the institution in which you are interested about enrolling in a course: most also have a mid-year intake, which means you may be able to start your course in June/July.

THE STRUCTURE OF A UNIVERSITY

Universities are generally large organisations that run courses at a number of different campuses. To a new student, it can all be very daunting and, until you make friends, a little lonely.

Within the large institution, a university has many different sections. Academic departments (schools, units or centres) are involved in running courses for students and/or undertaking research. You will get to know the lecturers in your department through classes and other activities. Each department has a head, who is usually an associate professor or professor. Different departments are generally grouped according to the same field of study: for instance, the faculty of engineering would include civil, electronic, electrical, mechanical and industrial engineering departments. The faculty is run by a dean and sometimes an assistant dean.

Administrative departments take care of the general business of academic departments and faculties. They organise student records, payments, administrative requests, scholarship matters and so on. There is a student administration section at most university campuses which takes care of enrolments, student cards and queries regarding leave, transfer of courses, withdrawal and graduation issues.

Each university has an academic board, which monitors the quality of teaching, research and the relationship between courses and departments, among other duties. This board is made up of senior management, heads of departments, deans and student representatives. Representatives from staff and students are elected through a university-wide voting system.

The vice-chancellor is responsible for the development of the university and is normally assisted by one or two deputy vice-chancellors. The chancellor of the university is a person of high merit in society and represents the university as the titular head. Figure 1.1 is a general, brief representation of the academic structure of a university.

Figure 1.1 Academic structure of a university

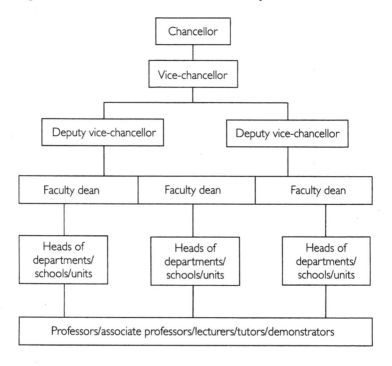

THE STRUCTURE OF A TAFE INSTITUTION

TAFE institutions are also generally large organisations, which run a wide range of courses at a number of different campuses and by distance learning. Courses are run during the day and evening and some are held on weekends.

The director of TAFE is responsible for the development of the different sections within the institution. Reporting to the director are the various heads of schools. Departments are involved in running courses for students, while units undertake a lot of collaborative project-type activity, for example with industry or other organisations. Each department has a head, who reports to the head of the school. As in universities, different departments are generally grouped according to field of study: for instance, the School of Business would normally include the accounting, hospitality and tourism and marketing departments.

Administrative departments take care of general business, such as student records, payments, administrative requests, accounting

Figure 1.2 Structure of a TAFE institution

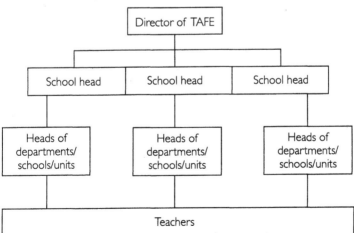

and finance. There is usually a student administration section at each TAFE institution which takes care of such issues as enrolments, student cards, queries regarding leave, transfer of courses and student withdrawals.

Each TAFE has a board, which looks at teaching and learning matters within the institution and is made up of various representatives of the institution. Figure 1.2 is a general, brief representation of the structure of a TAFE college.

UNIVERSITY-LEVEL QUALIFICATIONS

The *bachelor's degree* usually takes three or four years, while a bachelor's degree with *honours* takes an extra year. Once you have graduated from a bachelor's degree you have completed *undergraduate studies*. You can continue your studies by taking up a *postgraduate course*. *Graduate diplomas* or *postgraduate diplomas* take one year and usually are vocationally based, so may include a practice period in a work situation. A *master's degree* can include coursework, research or a combination of both, and takes one or two years to complete. Some universities offer a *doctoral degree*, which has a coursework component and a research component; this usually takes three years to complete full-time. A *PhD degree* usually takes a minimum of three years to complete also. Normally this course comprises research only and is the highest qualification at university level. All these courses are offered on a part-time basis, but you may need to check the time limitations for completion of courses with the coordinating lecturer at the university in which you are interested, as there are slight variations between institutions. Figure 1.3 is a general outline of how the qualifications system works in Australia.

Figure 1.3 Qualifications system in Australia

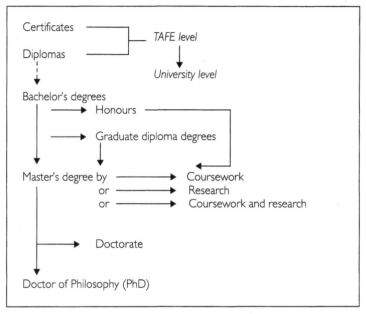

TAFE-LEVEL QUALIFICATIONS

Certificates are offered at four levels, while *diplomas* are offered also in vocational or applied fields of studies such as hospitality and tourism, computing, business, community and welfare services, engineering and technical sciences, planning and surveying, agriculture, architecture, art, craft or performance studies. These take from one to two years of full-time study and can be undertaken on a part-time basis. *Advanced diplomas* involve a third year of study. Depending on the course, students may be able to have their studies accredited to a university-level course. Transfers from TAFE to university, or vice versa, are also possible.

ENTRANCE EXAMS FOR INTERNATIONAL STUDENTS

As an international student you need to prove your competency in the English language before enrolling in a course. You must have one of the following:

- the equivalent of two years' successful full-time study at tertiary level, where English was the main language of instruction;
- a specified score on a recognised English language test (IELTS/TEOFL etc.);
- a Foundation Studies Certificate;
- an international baccalaureate minimum of Grade 5 in English as a higher-level subject in Group 1 Language A or Group 2 Language B.

You may need to achieve at least a specified score on an English language proficiency test before gaining access to an educational institution. The score sometimes depends on the course you choose, so you should check carefully. Also, be aware that the minimum score may change from year to year. Primarily, Australian educational institutions recognise the *IELTS* (International English Language Testing System) and the *TOEFL* (Test Of English as a Foreign Language). You can sit for these tests in your own country or in Australia. English language courses are available throughout the world which assist in preparing for these tests. Your teacher will be able to help you decide on your readiness to sit for the test.

A 'foundation course' is available in Australia and may also be available in your own country. This course is the equivalent of the last year of secondary school in Australia. It gives students the equivalent of a matriculation certificate and, on successful completion, equips them with the necessary qualifications to apply for a university course.

ELICOS CENTRES FOR INTERNATIONAL STUDENTS

ELICOS (English Language Intensive Courses for Overseas Students) centres are specially set up for international students who want to improve their English language skills. These centres run language courses at different levels, IELTS and TOEFL preparation courses, and English for academic purposes courses. Apart from language practice, the courses offer a useful insight into Australian culture and society, which is helpful when settling into a new country.

When selecting an ELICOS centre, choose carefully. The questions presented in the box below may help you in your selection.

CHOOSING AN ELICOS COURSE

- Does the centre have the course that I need?
- What does the course offer?
- Does the centre offer more advanced courses that I will need later on?
- Is there a student resource centre located on the premises that I can access? What does it contain?
- Does it have a social program as well as an academic program?
- If I am unable to pursue my studies, what are the refund procedures?
- Is there a student counsellor who can help me with accommodation problems or any personal matters that may arise?
- Is a prayer room available (if relevant)?

FEE-PAYING OR HECS-PAYING STUDENTS

Courses can be paid for in two ways, depending on the situation. Students who are Australian citizens can pay in advance. Here, each year the fee is paid (less a discount) before the cut-off date, which is usually the end of March. Alternatively, students can delay payment by applying for the Higher Education Contribution Scheme (*HECS*). Here, the repayment of fees will occur automatically when the student earns over a particular amount in salary, and repayment is collected through the taxation system. If a student is on a scholarship, he or she may not have to pay HECS.

There is a *full-fee-paying* option, which is open to international students as well as local students. In this case, students are required to pay for the whole cost of the course by the end of the enrolment period. The rules about this option vary between courses and institutions. You should check with the course coordinator, international office or student administration for precise details.

PRE-ENROLMENT DECISIONS

Choosing the right course

Choosing the right course is not always easy as it depends on different educational and vocational interests, entry scores and course availability. Institutions have course guides, while faculties, schools or departments have handbooks listing courses and any required prerequisites. Each faculty in a university has a handbook; TAFE also has handbooks. These are available online or in printed form from libraries or the institution bookshop. Take the time to review the courses that are offered at each institution to check that they suit your study plans.

The type of course you choose should suit your objectives and character. It may not be worth the effort of going through a medical degree if you do not really want a job that deals directly with people. However, it is a good idea to look at other options—that is, where a degree might lead. For instance, a medical degree may lead to a career in medical research, which may suit you better. It is important to get all the information about courses before you make a final decision.

Most courses have core subjects (which you must take) and a list of elective subjects from which you can choose. *Core subjects* cover fundamental knowledge and principles of a course, while *electives* allow you to choose subjects according to interest and objectives. If you have questions, talk to the course co-ordinator to get a better idea of course content and how it can help you succeed in your plans. A student adviser may also be able to help you with your selection.

Recognition of prior learning

This is a system that recognises a student's other studies and relevant work or life experience. If you, as a prospective student, can show the required level of competence, you may receive credits instead of having to undertake similar studies again. The course may then be taken in a shorter time than normally required. You should discuss this option with the coordinating lecturer of the selected course if you think you have already taken similar subjects or courses. Bring proof of these studies or experience to assist you in your discussions.

Distance learning

Some courses are offered by distance or flexible delivery mode. Distance education courses allow you to undertake a course using workbooks, videos and cassettes which are sent out to you. Now there is a trend to put courses on the Internet. Once you have enrolled for a course, you will be given instructions and a personal identification number (PIN) that will allow you to access course materials.

Withdrawing or deferring

If you decide to change your course, you can do so with the assistance of the department and student administration. You might need to withdraw and then enrol in another course. You can also defer one subject of a course or even the whole course. This means you delay studying the subject or course for a period of time. The course coordinator or international student adviser will be able to assist you with your queries.

If you find that a course is too difficult, or circumstances have changed and you need to withdraw from your studies completely for a while, you can make arrangements so that your academic record does not show a *fail* as a result. Student administration will help you organise this.

SUPPORT SERVICES

Special consideration

Sometimes health, family or other personal events affect your studies so that you are unable to submit all the work required, or your work suffers. Under these circumstances you are encouraged to speak to a lecturer, a student counsellor or an international student adviser. Together you may be able to devise some strategies that will help you with your studies. One strategy may be to submit a 'special consideration form', in which you request that the circumstances of the problem be considered in the assessment of an assignment, exam or overall progress.

Study skills courses

During the semester or semester breaks, institutions generally offer intensive study skills courses. These usually run for a week or two for students of the institution. The courses cover areas such as essay and report writing, grammar, research skills and critical thinking skills. Specific postgraduate or research intensive workshops are also held. These extra study skills courses offer students a chance to practise and develop skills, ask questions and get advice specifically on individual academic skills. Normally these courses are run by the academic skills support unit.

Academic skills support unit

Each institution has an academic skills support unit. This unit runs classes and workshops on aspects such as essay writing, researching, oral presentations, thesis preparation and time management. In addition, most run support classes for specific disciplines. The lecturers will be able to help you pinpoint areas that need improvement, as well as advise you on different strategies to help you develop the necessary skills and confidence to undertake your studies. The lecturers are there to help all students, so there is no need to feel uncomfortable about seeing someone. You can ask for your discussions to be kept confidential if this worries you. Lecturers are happy when students take the initiative to see them, so you should seek out advice and assistance if you need it.

Other services available

Each institution has a number of student and staff support services. Some are listed below.

Medical services

Australia has good-quality medical care. Both private and public hospitals cater for the needs of the community. General practitioners or doctors are located in most suburbs, so it is always easy to get medical assistance. You can discuss issues regarding any aspect of your health and wellbeing with a doctor in a confidential environment. If you wish, you can choose to see a female or male doctor. Most educational institutions have a medical service also. This may be staffed by a nurse or both a nurse and doctor. Some also have dentistry and optometry services. As a student you are entitled to access these services for no or minimal cost: just bring along your student and medical cards.

As an international student, you will be asked to pay a health care levy when you apply for your visa. You need to check *carefully* what this levy entitles you to as this may change periodically. You will also have an opportunity to take out private health cover to supplement your entitlements. Check with the Australian Embassy in your country for up-to-date information. Careful advance preparation can save you having to worry should you need medical treatment.

Chaplaincy

A chaplaincy is available to staff and students regardless of religious affiliation. Anglican, Jewish, Catholic, Orthodox, Muslim and other religious faiths are usually represented. Counselling, social and other activities are organised for students by the chaplaincy or related associations.

Counselling services

Counsellors are employed by every institution to assist staff and students with problems. In some cultures it is unusual and difficult to talk about such personal problems as finances, stress and disillusionment. However, without family and friends around you, you may prefer to speak to someone confidentially about particular worrying matters. Counsellors offer a *confidential* opportunity to listen and to talk as they help you work through concerns. Using this service is common and you should not feel embarrassed, ashamed or reluctant to take advantage of it.

Disability services

The disability officer provides information and assistance on services for students with any kind of disability. It is important to make contact with this person if you have a disability. Information on services that the institution offers will help you get the best out of your educational experience.

Equal opportunity

Equity is an important issue in Australia. Relationships between people are generally maintained on an equitable level. Educational institutions in Australia practise strict equal opportunity policies, which means that no student or staff member should be subjected to discrimination based on:

- gender
- race
- disability
- political beliefs
- pregnancy
- marital status
- sexual preference
- religion
- social position
- economic position.

Information on aspects of equal opportunity and any concerns you may have should be discussed with the equity officer.

Accommodation services

The housing officers assist students in obtaining suitable accommodation. Options may include student residences or halls, flats (apartments) and houses. When sharing or renting a place you will probably need to sign a tenancy agreement or pay a *bond*. This is a sum of money paid to the landlord or real estate agency in case rental is not received or repairs are not paid for by the tenants. The bond is returned if all is in order at the end of the rental agreement. It is a good idea to speak to the housing officer about such points. Dealing with agents on your own can be confusing, and the service offers helpful information and advice.

If you are an international student who would prefer to stay with a family, there is a *homestay service* that will arrange a placement for you. This can be arranged through the international office at the institution in which you enrol, before or after you arrive in Australia.

Scholarships and grants

Information on scholarships and grants can be obtained from the course coordinator, student administration or scholarships office. The amount and types available vary each year. If you are thinking about a scholarship or grant before you come to Australia, check with the Australian Education Centre in your country. Institutions also post information on their Web pages for local and overseas students.

Financial services

Advisers are available to assist with financial matters such as budgeting, getting a loan or other financial assistance. Sometimes a loan can be applied for through a student loan fund.

Useful associations

There are a number of associations and clubs that you can join or go to for information. These provide a great way of meeting people and releasing study stress. Some of them are listed below.

Overseas student association

This association represents the interests and concerns of overseas students and is normally run by them. By joining you will receive newsletters and invitations to social events such as discos, theatre nights, cultural events and trips. You will also get news about helpful study workshops.

Mature-aged students association

Sometimes, being older than many other students can make you feel isolated. The mature-aged students association arranges useful workshops and social events to help make the whole educational experience more pleasant and rewarding.

Bookshops

Bookshops are generally located on campus. These shops stock textbooks set as reading texts and other interesting books, stationery, software, newspapers and magazines. Second-hand bookshops on or near campus provide a useful service by buying used texts and selling them at a discounted price.

Clubs and associations

There are a number of associations and clubs that you can either join or refer to for information. The student union and post-graduate student association are among the associations set up to assist students. Sporting and special-interest clubs such as the computer club, film club and soccer club can be a great way of meeting people and releasing study stress.

Information on services, clubs and associations will be available throughout the year. A lot of institutions give out diaries that include this information during enrolment and orientation. Orientation week is another good opportunity to gather information and meet new people.

Orientation week

Orientation (or 'O-week') usually occurs a week before the first semester begins—that is, late February. Sometimes there is a smaller orientation program for students commencing mid-year. The week includes many social activities and information sessions. It is designed to give you an opportunity to ask questions, become familiar with your institution and make friends. Activities include:

- campus tours
- study skills seminars
- musical concerts
- information on clubs and associations
- competitions.

CONCLUSION

Educational institutions in Australia offer a range of academic courses and support services to help you obtain a comprehensive educational experience. It is important to get all the information on a course, fees and how a course assists your study plans before you make the final decision. While this will take some time, obtaining information will be made easier if you ask for advice and information from the relevant people or offices. The range of learning and social activities throughout the year can make your time at university not only scholary, but also enjoyable and enriching.

2

Choosing to study in Australia

Many students study in Australia to gain a good education in a relatively safe, clean and hospitable country. While the studies undertaken will help prepare a student for the future, the opportunity for self-development and experiencing life as an adult are also important aspects of the whole experience. During a period away from familiar surroundings, students will encounter unfamiliar aspects of life, of the education system, the food, the language, cultural ways and traditions. Homesickness and culture shock may be part of this experience but a sense of unfamiliarity is all part of the process of discovery. Living in a new country, surrounded by its culture, will mean learning to adapt and enjoy these differences.

Talking about relationships, feelings, cultural differences and other such aspects is always difficult as the discussion will necessarily include generalisations—that is, general views and stereotypes. So this should be taken into account when reading this chapter. Your own personality and views will contribute to the richness of your experiences. Nonetheless, the information and advice included in this chapter are based on the experiences of international students who have studied in Australia, and are aimed at helping other students to prepare for the big adventure ahead.

ACCOMMODATION

The International Office can usually organise accommodation for you with a family, a student hostel or in a student residence. Accommodation with a family is normally arranged through the Homestay Program. You should receive information on your accommodation arrangement options before you depart.

Student residences sometimes offer meals or have cooking facilities. Check to see if there are shared bathrooms or whether bathrooms are included in rooms. While most halls of residence are not segregated for males and females, they have their own separate bathrooms. Laundry facilities are normally located in student halls. Hostels are usually cheap options for accommodation. Check with the International Office regarding which ones are recommended, the costs, and the services (e.g. laundry and cooking) offered by each.

The housing officers at your institution will be able to help you find a place to share or rent on your own. Student noticeboards are other good sources of information.

Another option may be to try real estate agencies, which you will find located around the suburbs where you would like to live. These agencies have lists of flats and houses for rent and sale. Before using their services it is a good idea to speak to the housing officer or international student adviser at your institution about house/flat-hunting strategies.

You might like to remain with a *homestay family* for the length of your stay in Australia, or you could merely stay for a while to give you time that you need to get settled and make other arrangements.

Staying with a family

Staying with a family can be a rewarding and happy experience. The family can help you learn about cultural differences and will give you an opportunity to practise your language skills. Also, it will provide an opportunity to make friends in a new country.

It is important to be prepared for differences in the way people relate to each other and relate to you. You may find that your host family has different routines from those you are used to in your own family. For instance, you may find that everyone (including male members) is expected to take turns at washing the dishes, or that family members eat at different times, rather than come together at dinner time, due to work or other commitments. You may be confused at the different ways in which respect and family love are expressed between parents and children, brothers and sisters. For instance, teasing and joking are quite common—not only among brothers and sisters but parents too. Also, a husband and wife may hold hands in public as a sign of affection.

In some cultures the family stays together until the children marry. The children may then leave to set up their own homes. You may meet fellow students in Australia who come from cultural backgrounds where this is customary. On the other hand, you may meet students who have left home and are living alone or sharing a flat with friends. Often these students will have left home as young adults with parental agreement, as the parents may believe that it is time for their children to take up the responsibilities of adulthood. This is generally not a sign that the child is unloved, or has brought shame on the family and is unwanted. The respect and love between parents and children continue even when they do not all live in the same house.

Also, it is not unusual for students to have part-time jobs in order to help fund their studies. This does not necessarily mean that the parents are too poor, or do not want to assist their son or daughter in their studies, but is all about encouraging a sense of responsibility in their children.

Your host family may have a pet such as a dog or cat. It is generally thought that having a pet is positive—even therapeutic—as pets provide company and, through caring for them (feeding, washing, walking), children learn to take responsibility. Janelle, a Kenyan student, was staying with an Australian host family. She was surprised when she saw that her host family allowed the children to play with and even wash the dog. She was horrified that it was allowed into the house, particularly when it tried to sit on her lap. She later remarked that the dog was treated as part of the family. Her experience of dogs in Kenya was of dirty animals with diseases, therefore not to be touched. The host family, realising she was not comfortable with the dog, asked Janelle whether she was scared of dogs and she explained her views on the subject. In the end, both Janelle and her host family learnt something about the different attitudes Australians and Kenyans have to animals, and a compromise was reached. Whatever the problem, it usually helps to talk about it to save embarrassment and confusion.

Each family has its own ways, and Australia is a multicultural country. As a result, you may find that your host family represents a mixed cultural background—perhaps Vietnamese Australian, Irish Australian or Greek Australian. You may learn about a variety of cultures and this mixture will make your own experience unique.

If you are having problems adapting to life with a particular family, you should talk to them about this. Sometimes misunderstandings are cleared up quickly by simple explanation, as in the case of Janelle. If there is a more complicated problem, seek the advice of the international officer at your institution, who will either be able to help clarify matters or help you find a more suitable family. The important thing is to speak out if you are unhappy about a situation.

At the airport

Arriving at the airport can be a daunting experience if you are not prepared. When you are making final arrangements for your course you can arrange for someone to 'meet and greet' you. A representative will be waiting at the airport with your name on a big card so that you can easily identify him or her. The representative will take you to your chosen accommodation. Alternatively, there are 'shuttle' buses that go from the airport to the city centre at regular intervals, stopping at some hotels along the way. Inform the bus driver of where you need to go.

WORKING IN AUSTRALIA

At present, overseas students are permitted to work part-time, up to a maximum of 20 hours per week. However, work is not always easy to find. Your institution will have a list of part-time and casual work positions available. Also, you can check for vacancies in newspapers or by talking to other students. Students often take up a variety of jobs such as tutoring, restaurant work and retail work. They find that getting a job not only adds to their income but also to their experience of life in Australia.

SETTLING-IN PROBLEMS

Homesickness

Feeling homesick is a normal part of finding yourself in a strange country away from your family and friends. Everything is so strange—even the language. You might feel homesick after hearing a song that reminds you of your friends or home. Sometimes homesickness will make you cry for a few minutes, or it might depress you for a period of weeks. It is important to recognise these feelings of homesickness. Do not think you are being childish or silly or that you are not able to cope. You should not blame yourself for missing your friends and family, but it is important to try not to let these feelings interfere with enjoying the positive aspects of being in a different country and making new friends. The ironic thing about this feeling is that you may even feel homesick when you return home after your studies and are missing your Australian friends and being in Australia.

Culture shock

Sometimes homesickness is linked to culture shock. You may be confused by many aspects of your new environment—strange customs, strange foods, strange language, strange dress, strange behaviour. This can be quite stressful. Even though Australia has a British history which influences many facets of society such as the legal and parliamentary system, Australian culture is dramatically different in some respects. Thus, even students from the UK or USA can experience culture shock.

Negative feelings against your new environment are evident in statements such as 'the weather is too changeable' , 'the people eat too much bread' or 'the tomatoes aren't as tasty as at home'. While comparing two cultures is natural and logical, constant negativity towards the new culture will not assist the process of adjustment.

Culture shock can cause headaches, moodiness, insomnia (inability to sleep), stomach aches, loss of appetite and so on. It can make you feel quite alienated and isolated from your fellow classmates. Some students have described it as feeling as if they are in a bubble—that they are in a group of people but feel lonely, distant and alien. However, it is important that you do attempt to make friends and you will soon realise that there is nothing 'wrong' with you. Some universities set up a mentor scheme, so that you may be 'guided' by another overseas student who has been in Australia for a while who understands your feelings. The international student officer can assist you if you are feeling particularly low and upset about the new environment, as can be seen in the following case study of John.

CASE STUDY: JOHN

John, a South African student, came to Australia feeling very excited about all the new opportunities he would have. He got on well with his studies and made new friends. He missed his family a little. After a few months however, he began to feel so confused and alienated by his new surroundings that he began to feel ill and stopped attending classes regularly. He fell behind in his studies and his marks dropped. He received a letter advising him of an appointment that had been made for him to see his lecturer and the international student adviser. At the meeting, he was asked to explain his non-attendance and poor performance. During the discussion, John's distress became obvious. He said he felt isolated, unmotivated in his studies and wanted to go home, but could not do so because it would be regarded by his community as shameful to return home without completing his studies. When he was asked why he had not gone to see the international student adviser earlier, he explained that in his culture going to see an adviser was an unfamiliar idea, and that *counselling* was undertaken only for people who had psychiatric problems. Also, the adviser was female, and this would be inappropriate. According to his customs he should sort out his own problems and certainly not speak to a woman about them.

A number of issues are raised by John's situation. His feelings of culture shock and unfamiliarity with the role of a student counsellor prevented him from seeking assistance, but each culture has its own way of dealing with things. If John had had a problem at home he would have had someone to talk to. John had not been in Australia long enough to have made a trusted friend. His high expectations of himself for his studies and to make his family and community proud of him became stressful. John needed to lessen the stress he put on himself. Also, he was not aware of the many different roles and types of advisory and counselling services available in Australia, and that it is common, accepted practice to speak to someone in order to get advice and work out strategies. In addition, it is not uncommon in Australia for students to see an adviser of a different gender—it is acceptable for students to ask to see either a male or female counsellor, depending on their preference.

After culture shock was discussed at the meeting, John began to understand that his was a normal and understandable reaction to a country so different from his own. A study plan was worked out for him so he could redo an assignment and catch up on others. Arrangements were made for him to see a male student adviser, who helped John understand some of the aspects of studying and living in Australia he was confused about. He also organised for John to meet other students and join social events. For John, it was important to *recognise his feelings* and not to feel he was weak because of them.

Adjusting to a different culture means that you will experience different ideas, foods, types of relationships and behaviour. Keeping a diary is one way of expressing your feelings about and reactions to your new environment. It is important not to get angry at yourself or at others because of your feelings. Keep up a good routine, get up at a reasonable hour and attend your classes, do some exercise, eat well and avoid *junk food* (food that is not nutritious). Relax in your favourite way, for instance by watching a video, jogging or visiting places. Do not be afraid to get some advice: the student advisers or counsellors are employed by the institutions specifically to help *you*.

Socialising in Australia

You may also encounter differences in the way people socialise in Australia. To some cultures, the Australian way of socialising seems odd and very informal. For example, after a dinner at a friend's house it is considered common courtesy to help wash the dishes after a meal, even if you are male. Your offer may not be accepted, but it is polite to offer. It is also common to go to parties and restaurants in casual dress such as jeans, unless there is a 'dress code'.

The dress code in Australia can be different from what you are used to. Australians are generally quite informal in their dress. You will notice that office workers dress in suits or smart dresses but at university the code varies. Students generally wear jeans, T-shirts, shirts and jumpers. Shorts are quite acceptable, along with sandals and other casual footwear. You may be surprised to find that some lecturers wear jeans also. Relatively few pieces of jewellery are worn and expensive jewellery is kept for special occasions. During your stay you may be invited to a formal gathering. Normally, formal wear involves wearing a suit, a shirt with a collar and tie for men and formal dresses or suits for women.

It is quite common for a group of people to get together at someone's house for a birthday party, barbecue (BBQ) or a gathering, each bringing their own drinks and sometimes contributing a plate of food. It is particularly common to bring a bottle of wine to a dinner party (see the case study below of Huynh and Van).

CASE STUDY: HUYNH AND VAN

Huynh and Van came from Vietnam and were very excited when they got an invitation to a fellow student's birthday party. At the bottom of the invitation they noticed it said 'BYO drinks and plate'. They asked their English teacher what this meant and, at first, felt insulted when it was explained that BYO meant *bring your own*. Doing this in Vietnam would be an insult to the guest, who expects that the host family share their food and drink as this represents a special form of respect towards the guest. In Vietnam it is expected that the guest will invite the host at a later date to repay the hospitality. Also, for guests to bring food and drink would be offensive to the host, as it would imply that the host was not capable of providing nice food or drink for the guests.

Speaking to Huynh and Van, it was explained that BYO is a custom in Australia and that, while the host provides some food and drink, everyone shows their respect by contributing a plate of food or drink. Also, it is quite usual for the guest to ask what the host requires so that not everyone brings the same things. Not every party is BYO: usually it is for more informal gatherings. Once this was explained Huynh and Van did not feel insulted and soon organised their own BYO party.

Food differences

Being a multicultural country, Australia has access to all sorts of food and ingredients for cooking. Supermarkets and markets stock a variety of vegetables, fruits, herbs and spices which make it easy to cook any type of recipe. In Australia it is common to eat pork, beef and veal (where religious beliefs permit). Halal meat, kosher and other specially prepared foods are normally easily available. If *your* religious beliefs mean that you cannot eat a certain food, inform your host beforehand and your beliefs will be respected. Vegetarian meals are commonly served, but you can check to make sure.

DEVELOPING INDEPENDENT LEARNING SKILLS

At tertiary level a lot more is expected of a student, and these expectations are not necessarily detailed for you. For instance, you may be required to write a report without ever having written one before, and your lecturers may not go into much detail about what such a task entails. Thus, students need to develop independent learning skills. Such skills will include an ability to question and research—that is, to seek out relevant sources of information and assistance.

Maria's experience (see the case study on the next page) seems typical of the general student experience. Maria learnt to ask questions and seek assistance. She demonstrated good independent

CASE STUDY: MARIA FROM SWITZERLAND

When I first entered my class I felt nervous. There were lots of students and I didn't know any of them. The tasks the lecturer gave us were interesting but I didn't have a clue where to start. I went to the library and felt so confused about what to do. I left again and went home. A few days later I overheard some students talking about getting some books out of the closed-reserve section of the library. I decided to try again. I was a bit nervous about my English language skills, but I asked a librarian who was very helpful. I worked with the material and drew up an outline. I compared this to examples of other business reports and then made an appointment to see my lecturer. I explained that I had never written such a report before. She kindly answered the questions I had prepared and told me I was on the right track.

learning skills. After her initial confusion, she sought out relevant information to help her with her assignment. She prepared her questions and asked for assistance. By the time Maria finished her course she had developed a sense of confidence in her own ability to seek out and get the information she needed, she felt more confident in approaching people and did not wait to overhear clues.

Just like journalists, students need to develop skills and confidence to ask the basic six questions: Who? Where? What? When? How? and Why? As you read, discuss or listen you will come across the answers, and probably more questions. This is all part of the learning process which makes learning fun instead of a chore.

RELATIONSHIPS WITH LECTURERS AND PEERS

The teaching staff you meet will introduce themselves, generally, by the name they want to be referred to. Do not be surprised if they expect you to use their first name. Australians are generally informal, and it is common for students and lecturers to refer to each other by their first names. You may feel uncomfortable with this if you come from a background where titles and surnames are used, or where terms such as 'madam' and 'sir' are used to demonstrate respect. However, in Australia these terms are considered very old-fashioned, if not impolite. Watch and listen to how other students address the lecturers and you can do the same. Using the first name will not be considered disrespectful if that is what your lecturers prefer.

Discussing your work with lecturers is normal—in fact, it is considered strange if a student does not approach lecturers from time to time to ask questions. For instance, you may, while doing preparatory reading for an essay, find that some ideas are unclear or unexpected. It is entirely appropriate then to make an appointment to see your lecturer to clarify the ideas. If it is a quick question you may be able to ask the lecturer before or after a class. While in some cultures asking questions may be considered disrespectful of the lecturer's authority, in Australia it is a sign of respect for the role of a teacher.

Meeting new people and making new friends can be exciting and fun, but developing a relationship takes time. In Australia, for example, talking about the weather is considered a friendly thing to do when people do not know each other very well. This involves no personal questions—such as questions about someone's weight or age—which are considered to be inappropriate when people do not know each other very well. Also, questions such as why a married person does not have children, why someone is not married and how much a person earns are considered private topics in Australia although in some countries such questions are part of polite conversation when getting to know someone.

Male–female relationships

Generally men and women relate in a friendly way and socialise as friends, on an equally respectful basis. They go to parties, a movie or meet on campus for lunch as friends. Conversations can be merely friendly and joking or can touch on serious matters such as family, study or other issues. As Australia is made up of people from different ethnic backgrounds, there is a general respect for, and acceptance of, the fact that in some cultures male–female friendships are uncommon. Once you feel comfortable you will be able to find a way to join in activities and conversations in a way in which you feel comfortable.

Friendships sometimes evolve into closer or more intimate relationships. This can be a wonderful experience, getting to know another person, treating each other as special and developing a warm relationship. If, however, the relationship begins to cause anxiety and stress and to affect your studies or health, you should think about getting some advice from friends or even a counsellor. It can be easier to talk to a counsellor, who will be non-judgmental and offer confidential support.

LANGUAGE

You may have studied English for a number of years in your own country and still find that, in an academic environment where English is the native language, your skills need some further work. Sometimes the accent, idioms and general oral language are unfamiliar: as an overseas student you may have practised English mainly through books and exams. However, being involved in an environment where English is used around you constantly (on TV, radio, in classes) will lead you to develop your skills to a level where you feel confident with your abilities to understand and contribute.

Support is available through an academic skills unit at your institution, which will assist you with developing academic skills in such areas as essay writing, oral presentations, exam preparation and grammar. Workshops are organised throughout the year, including break times, and often individual appointments can be made.

If extra language assistance is needed, there are many reputable English language centres in Australia. These offer a range of courses, from general English to English for academic purposes, and IELTS or TOEFL courses. Some centres are independent, while others are part of a higher education institution. It is important to research the services and types of courses offered by the centres in which your are interested. It would be worthwhile enrolling in a course to develop your language skills as well as your cultural understanding of Australia (see also chapter 1).

Courtesies

In Australia, omitting the words 'please' and 'thank you' is considered discourteous, although these words may be used in different circumstances in your native language. It is important to learn how not to make a bad impression. For example, you are expected to say 'thank you' when someone assists you, as in a shop when the assistant sells you a book and you are paying for the item. Also, as everyone is treated equally, it is as important to be polite to a waiter or a receptionist as to a professor—otherwise you may find you get poor service or no service at all.

You might also notice the frequent use of the conditional tense (*would, could, may*). In English, the conditional plays a very important role as it turns a command or a statement into a polite request. Consider the differences in the following:

The menu!	May I have a menu please? Thank you.
Where are the toilets?	Could you please tell me where the toilets are?
Photocopy this for me.	Would you photocopy this for me, please?
I want a bus ticket.	May I have a bus ticket?
Move your chair.	Would you mind moving your chair?

Australian idioms

Australians have their own way of using language. The Australian accent is different from the English or American one and 'slang' or idiom is common. Slang is made up of words or phrases that are common in everyday spoken language but are not standard English and are inappropriate in written form, except in personal, friendly correspondence. If you have seen *Crocodile Dundee* or *Neighbours* in English you may have heard some slang already such as 'fair dinkum' to mean 'truly'. You will probably pick up and use some of this idiom during your stay. Some of the more common phrases and words have been listed in appendix 1, so you can start practising.

Body language

Communication occurs not only through oral and written language but also through body language. However body language differs from culture to culture and can be confusing. Watch people to see how body language is expressed but do not try repeating a gesture until you are sure of its meaning.

Eye contact

Maintaining eye contact is important during conversation with peers, lecturers in tutorials and in oral presentations. Eye contact demonstrates honesty, openness, agreement and willingness to engage in discussion. In some African and Asian cultures, eye contact can indicate disrespect, arrogance and disagreement, and some students find it difficult to adjust. They will attempt to maintain eye contact and giggle because they are uncomfortable. Or they may giggle and look away if they are expressing an opposite view or talking about something negative or sad. The limited eye contact may make the listener think the student is uninterested, and the giggling may be seen as an indication of not being taken seriously.

TABOOS

The following are some common taboos, or habits that are seen as offensive, rude or insulting by most Australians. If you want to make a good impression, it is best to avoid these habits.

- *Sniffing* instead of blowing your nose is considered rude. In Australia it is common to see people using handkerchiefs or tissues to blow their noses. This is not considered unclean as it is in some cultures.
- *Constant clearing of the throat* is thought to be rude.
- *Spitting* in public is considered to be offensive, while in some countries it is a common thing to do. A person who spits in the street may get an insulted look, or even be fined for polluting.
- *Slurping soup* or making a noise when eating is thought to be rude. Eating in a public place should be done quietly.
- As in many countries, *dropping litter* (rubbish) or leaving it behind is considered impolite and is punishable with a fine.

Other things that are considered impolite are:

- opening someone's door without knocking first and waiting for the person to answer 'come in';
- going through a door without holding it open for the person behind you;
- arriving late for an appointment. If you are running late it is best to ring and advise the person;
- not arriving for an appointment. Cancel the appointment if it is not convenient or is no longer required.

Finally, *personal cleanliness* is held in high regard. Taking a shower or bath every day is a common practice.

CONCLUSION

By planning ahead you will be better prepared for your study adventure in Australia. You should investigate accommodation options and language training. Reading books about Australia will give you an idea of the different cultural environment but the best preparation is a positive, realistic attitude. If you are prepared for differences (some of which you may not like), are ready to enjoy the experience as a whole and keep a sense of humour and optimism, then it should all turn out to be a pleasant learning and life adventure.

3

Participating in classes

Actively participating in classes is an important part of being a successful student. This means being a good listener, thinking critically about the information and using it to build on your knowledge. This chapter describes the types of classes in which you might participate as part of your studies and aspects of involvement in these classes.

During your studies you may attend a number of different types of classes: lectures, tutorials, workshops, seminars, laboratory sessions/practical classes or 'pracs' and field trips. The types of classes you are required to attend depends on your course: for example, science and engineering courses include workshops and laboratory sessions.

Once you have a timetable you are expected to be self-disciplined and manage your time and studies. You are expected to be independent and seek out the information you need from libraries or community sources. Independence also means to be able to take the information you gain from your studies and life experiences in order to formulate your own ideas on an issue or problem. Tutorials, workshops and seminars are especially helpful because they allow you time to *discuss* issues, try out ideas and gather further information from your colleagues and lecturers. It is important to take advantage of these sessions and use them to discuss the ideas presented in lectures.

LECTURES

Lectures are usually different from tutorials. Some lectures are attended by hundreds of students and the lecturer delivers the information in a more formal way than in tutorials. Usually lectures last for one hour. Sometimes they explain the reading or present alternative opinions from researchers in the field. It is important to attend lectures in order to understand the issues relevant to the course, and also to get information on course assignments or exams. Often there is little or no time for students to ask questions during lectures, so issues raised during lectures are taken up for discussion in tutorials. It is important therefore to take clear notes that will help you remember the main points.

Note-taking is greatly assisted by preparation. Prepare for your lectures by thinking about the topic. See where each lecture fits into the course outline and how it links up with your other lectures. Think about what sort of information you would expect the lecturer to cover. Do your preliminary reading as the lecturer may go over the main points and help clarify the reading. You will also be in a better position to follow the argument if any contrary opinions are presented.

Arriving at lectures early means you will get a good seat and have time to get yourself ready for note-taking before you start. It may also mean you do not miss out on any handouts. During the lecture, you may be given a copy of notes that you can follow during the class and to which you can add brief comments as you listen to the lecturer.

Overhead slides are often used as outlines of main points and these will help guide your listening and understanding. Copies of overheads or slides may also be distributed. If the lecturer does not distribute a copy of a useful overhead, it is quite acceptable to speak to him/her after class and request a copy.

Each lecturer will have his or her own style of speaking, accent and body language. You will get used to a lecturer's style after a couple of sessions. Voice and pace are also used to emphasise points. English speakers usually slow down and raise their voice slightly when speaking in order to draw attention to an important point. You will get used to this as you proceed with your studies.

Listening is a very important skill for effective study. It is difficult to concentrate for a long time, particularly if English is not your first language. However, over a period of time, and as you get used to the language, accent and style of the lecturer, it will be easier to follow classes. Listen carefully to the lecture as important points will be emphasised in order to help you with your study of the subject. Phrases such as those listed in the box below help to signal important points:

PHRASES TO LISTEN OUT FOR

- remember that . . .
- a cause of . . .
- it is important/essential to note . . .
- a major aspect of . . .
- it must be remembered that . . .

- it is significant that . . .
- a major point . . .
- an important development in the area of . . .
- a result of . . .
- importantly . . .
- firstly, secondly . . .

Taping lectures

Try to resist taping all your lectures. Using your own listening skills is much more effective. Also, you will probably not have time to listen to the tapes of all of your lectures and take notes.

Choose to record only specific lectures, and then only when you have to.

TUTORIALS

A lecture may be attended by all the students of the course, while a tutorial comprises of a small group of students who, with a lecturer, work through tasks based on the lecture theme. These tasks may be based on reading, or a set of questions, or both. The group can range from 8 to 15 students, usually meeting once or twice a week. The tutorial is an opportunity to *discuss* issues presented in the lecture and reading. It is an opportunity to ask and answer questions. A tutorial is usually informal and gives the lecturer an opportunity to assist you in your interpretation of ideas and check your progress. It is important to engage in the discussion in tutorials. In Australia this is not considered impolite or disrespectful to the authority of the lecturer. Coming up with your own ideas, conclusions and questions demonstrates that you are thinking about the subject. Silence may indicate that you are too shy or that you have no ideas on the subject, are bored or uninterested.

DISCUSSIONS

During your studies you will be expected to take part in discussions. At first students usually feel shy and awkward about expressing opinions and asking questions because they feel they may risk making fools of themselves in front of their fellow students and lecturer. However, once students settle into the course they are expected to participate by answering and asking questions. It is important to be confident about speaking up in class, even if, from a cultural perspective, you find the situation strange—that is, disagreeing with the text or asking questions of the lecturer. After a while how to interact in a tutorial will become more familiar and you will feel confident about sharing your ideas or asking questions as part of class discussions. Talking too much is just as undesirable as not talking at all: if you have a tendency to be talkative you will need to learn to give others a chance to engage in class discussions.

If you are not confident of your English language skills and this holds you back, you may need to employ some strategies. Discussing issues with a friend before class to practise terms, pronunciation and the flow of words is helpful. Write down a few notes in case you get nervous and forget what you want to say, or to help you recall terms and expressions. Another strategy is to start slowly and build up your confidence over a period of time.

The role of questioning

While in some countries, education practices place a strong emphasis on learning by memory, in Australia the emphasis is on questioning. This is why in tutorial discussions students present opposing views and sometimes question the literature. For example, a discussion on the role of the family in society does not require a mere summary of information gained through classes and readings on this perspective—it requires the student to consider the aspects of the question. For instance:

- What society is being referred to?
- How is a family unit defined?
- Does a family unit include only a mother, father and children?
- What about single parents and children?
- Why has the role of the extended family changed?

Thinking critically about the information that is presented in classes and your reading is a similar process. It means you are not just passively absorbing the material but are using it to develop a fuller understanding of the complex issues related to your study area. By thinking critically you will be able to better participate in discussions. The *why, what, who, how, when, where* questions will be useful tools in your critical thinking (see box on the next page).

THINKING CRITICALLY

- What is the main argument?
- What evidence or theories are used to support the argument?
- How does the information fit with what I already know about the topic?
- Which questions are raised but not answered by the information presented?
- What can I read to enhance my understanding of the argument?
- Why is this an important topic?
- Where can I find out more on this topic?

LABORATORY SESSIONS/PRACTICAL CLASSES

Usually students involved in science and engineering classes have *lab* or *prac sessions* with lab technicians or demonstrators. These classes are valuable, as they allow students the opportunity to use specialised equipment to undertake experiments, drawings, mathematical procedures and to practise important research and technical skills.

FIELD TRIPS

Field trips may be part of the course you take. These involve going on an organised excursion to a particular place to investigate, in person, some of the issues, materials or objects you have been discussing in the course. For example, if you are studying the environment, there may be a field trip to a rainforest to observe the wildlife of the area; if you are studying art, there may be a field trip to a gallery to see a particularly interesting exhibition. Sometimes trips take two or three days, and are called *camps*.

WORKSHOPS

A workshop is usually attended by a small group of students and a tutor or lecturer. Similar to a tutorial, it is a time to discuss issues brought up in a lecture or to practise skills.

SEMINARS

Seminars are discussion groups in which each student takes a turn at giving a small presentation on an issue. The presentation becomes the basis for group discussion. Questions are asked, comments and suggestions are made. Postgraduate students may even be asked to present at a seminar. It is a good way of getting feedback on your work and checking that you are on the right track.

STUDY GROUPS

Study groups are often a great way to share ideas in an informal atmosphere—say, over coffee or a bowl of noodles. Students in the same course can come together to ask each other questions, put forward opinions on topics and prepare tutorial activities. Some study groups are advertised on department noticeboards or announced at tutorial meetings, or you can organise one yourself. A small group of interested students and a common time and place are all that is needed.

CONCLUSION

Whichever type of class you attend, to be a successful student you will need to do some preparation. Reread your previous class notes and read the main course texts and any other suggested material. Ensure that you complete the tutorial tasks. Critical thinking is important while you are reading and undertaking tasks. Have questions ready and be prepared to engage in class discussion.

4

Note-taking skills

Taking notes is an important part of tertiary studies as it helps you remember important issues. The amount of note-taking necessary will depend on the course. You will find that you will take notes:

- to prepare for essays;
- to prepare for exams;
- to record important details presented in class;
- to record essential points from your reading.

Different study styles mean that students have their own methods of note-taking, using individual recording systems, abbreviations, presentation and so on. There are many methods you can use, but it is important to get into the habit of good note-taking to make studying easier.

Note-taking is a way of recording the *main* ideas to assist you to remember key points. It also helps to get the important arguments of the course into perspective. Notes can be used for the preparation of assignments and exams. They allow you to record your own ideas using your own words and to compare them to ideas presented in a class or in reading texts.

Taking notes in a class requires a different technique from taking notes from reading material. In class you need to listen while taking notes and it is not always appropriate to interrupt and ask for an earlier point to be repeated. In note-taking from reading, you have static material you can review and check (e.g. vocabulary) but there is usually a lot of reading to do and time is limited.

Jargon

Note the jargon used in your area of study. Jargon is vocabulary that is used in a particular way and means something to specialists in a field. Think about how 'virus' is used in reference to computers compared to medicine, or how 'organisational behaviour' is used in business as compared to anthropology. Listing jargon and meanings can be a useful way of becoming familiar with it. Place the list on your study wall, the fridge or anywhere you will be able to see and think about it often.

Summarising notes

Writing a short summary at the end of your notes can assist your memory and thought processes. Synthesising the main arguments will also help you when reviewing your notes in preparing for an essay or exam: you can turn straight to the synthesis which will provide an overview of the arguments. Encircling this summary or highlighting it in coloured pen will help identify it quickly in your notebook.

Study groups

Study groups often provide a good opportunity to compare notes and discuss points that have arisen. If you do not catch or understand something that was said in a class, the other members of the study group can assist in clarifying the points.

> *Study tip* *Baroque music has been found to be very relaxing, allowing you to study while cutting off the sounds of the world outside.*

TAKING NOTES IN A CLASS

In a class it is important to listen and watch. This is difficult if you are busily taking down most of the information presented. It is better to concentrate on what the lecturer is saying and jot down the main points rather than to take down every word. Listening is an active process and sometimes you have to work hard on concentrating for an hour or more. However, good listening and note-taking will help you in your studies.

Note-taking involves jotting down (writing) key words, short phrases, questions and points. Your notes will be more meaningful as a summary rather than a word-for-word account of the class. You will probably develop your own abbreviations as you practise this skill. A list of common note-taking abbreviations has been adapted in appendix 2.

Ruling a generous margin on one side of the page allows you to add your own notes alongside the class notes when you read over your notes afterwards. You can add any thoughts, questions and issues that relate to your reading. In this way, your class notes become a useful working document and you have the chance to concentrate and think about the ideas presented in class. Reading the texts on your prescribed reading list will assist you in following the information presented by the lecturer.

Moreover, rereading notes after a class assists in facilitating memory and in critical thinking. If English is not your first language, under the pressure of note-taking in a class situation a word or phrase will sometimes come to you in your native language. Instead of spending time thinking of the equivalent English word and missing the next main point, write it down in your native language and sort out the English equivalent when you are rereading your notes after the class.

Overheads are often used by lecturers to highlight main points. Some students find that they are too busy copying them down to concentrate on what the lecturer says so that the notes become useless. Not all the information should be copied down as notes. Think about what is being presented and note down important points later (see Figure 4.1).

Recording classes

The taping of classes is sometimes arranged by the lecturer, or you may do it yourself although it is important to ask permission. Students who have English as a second language might tape several of the first few classes, particularly when adjusting to the accent. As the student gets used to being immersed in an English-speaking, academic environment, there is no longer any need to continue taping classes. It then becomes easier and less time-consuming to concentrate on the main points of the class and make appropriate written notes. Also, taping tends to double your workload and few of us have time for that!

TAKING NOTES IN A TUTORIAL, WORKSHOP OR LABORATORY SESSION

In practical classes a lot more goes on: listening, watching and doing. In these sessions you will probably take notes of the important things your teacher mentions as well as interesting aspects that come up as you work. You should not forget those important bits of information regarding methodology and theory so have an organised notebook ready.

Do not worry about new vocabulary as it is better to concentrate on getting the general meaning. Jot down unknown words or phrases in the margin to look up or ask about after the class.

Figure 4.1 Sample of note page

Course: Business Marketing

Week 4   **Lecturer:** Anthony Christopher

Lecture: Business Plans   **Date:** 10 May 2000

BP's essential strategy:

➡ 5-year plan

➡ 10-year plan

?

established co.
new co.–different
strategies for
developing a
business plan

Sections:

1 Executive summary

2 Environmental analysis

3 SWOT analysis

4 Alternatives

5 Objectives

6 Analysis

7 Recommendations

8 Measurement

9 Control and evaluation

Study tip   *Keep your notes neat and organised in a folder. Write your notes on looseleaf folder paper so that you are unlikely to lose them.*

TAKING NOTES TO PREPARE AN ASSIGNMENT

When preparing for an assignment, you will be required to select relevant material and use this material in a way that supports your argument. The lecturer will gauge whether you understand the arguments of authorities in your field. As you are reading you should keep in mind the critical reading skills listed in the box below.

CRITICAL READING SKILLS

- Is the information relevant to your essay topic?
- What are the arguments that are being presented and how are these supported?
- How does the information correlate with what has been presented in the course?
- How does it fit in with your own thoughts and experiences?
- How does it fit in with other reading you have done?
- If there is no agreement between this reading and your course notes, reading or experiences, what are the contrary issues and what evidence is presented to support the contrary argument?
- Who is the author? Is he or she a well-known specialist in the field?

Recording sources

When taking notes for an assignment, record the sources on a *resources record sheet* or index cards as you go along. The record sheet should be a separate section in your notebook, and this will become your bibliography. It will save time hunting down the information later. A record sheet has been reproduced in appendix 3 for you to copy.

Index cards can be stored in alphabetical order easily which is an advantage if you use many resources. These cards should

Figure 4.2 Sample index card

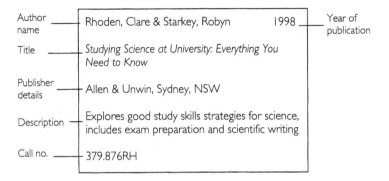

Author name	Rhoden, Clare & Starkey, Robyn	1998	Year of publication
Title	*Studying Science at University: Everything You Need to Know*		
Publisher details	Allen & Unwin, Sydney, NSW		
Description	Explores good study skills strategies for science, includes exam preparation and scientific writing		
Call no.	379.876RH		

contain the same information as the record sheet but be set out a little differently, though, of course, everyone has their own style. Figure 4.2 is an example.

TAKING NOTES FROM READING

It is important to keep in mind the purpose of your reading while you are note-taking. If you are reading to prepare for an essay, report or case study, keep the topic in mind and read relevant information. Try not to be distracted by interesting but irrelevant information.

It helps to read a section before taking notes so that you have a clear idea of the argument. Then you can note down the main points easily. At the top of the page you will need to add the full reference: that is, the author's full name, the title, date, publisher and place published. As you take notes, jot down the page numbers of any particular idea you record in your notebook. *Headings* are useful as they help organise issues on the page and flag certain bits of information when you are reading your notes.

Use your own words. They are *your* notes so only *you* need to understand them. However, do not take notes just because the words sound important. You need to be able to reflect on what you write down for the notes to be useful.

> **Study tip** *Take notes in your own words. If you need to quote, do not forget to reference.*

The presentation of notes is always important. Ensure that you write the date, topic, lecturer's name, week and page number clearly at the top of the page. This will help you keep an organised record of your notes. Try not to crowd the page with lots of writing, as you may want to add some details when you reread your notes after the lecture.

Afterwards you can also add any details that will help in understanding any issues raised. Some students use a different-coloured pen for underlining or use an asterisk (*) to highlight an important point. You will develop your own style, but try to concentrate on meaningful rather than pretty note-taking.

CONCLUSION

You will develop your own style of note-taking, one that suits your learning style and the course you are doing. Notes are for personal use, a working document to be referred to throughout the course. They need to reflect the main issues explored in the course—in classes, tutorial discussions and reading—as well as your own ideas.

✓ CHECKLIST FOR NOTE-TAKING

☐ Record the appropriate details at the top of the page.

☐ Include references and page numbers.

☐ Write clearly.

☐ Leave space so that you can add details when reviewing notes.

- [ ] Focus on the topic and record only the important points.
- [ ] Review your notes when you have finished.
- [ ] Use abbreviations—ones you will remember.
- [ ] Highlight key words and phrases.
- [ ] Rule a margin for your own comments and questions.
- [ ] Write a brief summary of the notes.
- [ ] Think about how the ideas in your notes relate to the other information in the course.

5

Reading at tertiary level

Your lecturer will probably give you a list of recommended texts and/or a book of readings and a list of additional, useful sources. Copies of the texts referred to are usually kept in the library, bought at the institution bookshop or other book stores. Your lecturers will let you know where you can locate important texts, or if you have any problems finding materials you should ask them for advice. In addition to the texts suggested, you will be expected to read other material in your field, to familiarise yourself with important arguments and different points of view. Consequently, you may find yourself a little bewildered at the amount and range of reading you are required to do as part of your course. Good reading strategies will help you get through it and to be prepared for assignments and classes.

CHOOSING READING MATERIAL

Textbooks, journal articles, internet publications and newspapers are all useful reading materials. When reviewing material to help you prepare an assignment or for general reading purposes, you need to examine its relevance, its date and its place in the context of the whole course. If you are examining a text to decide whether it is useful for your reading purposes, a look at headings, sub-headings, figures and tables should give you a good indication of what is in the text in the first instance. While the title gives you an indication of what the text is about, the contents and index pages act as more detailed guides. On the copyright page (at the back of the title page) you will find a date of publication and information on editions or reprinting. As a general rule, if the text is dated more than six years ago, it may not be as useful as more contemporary works. However, reprints or multiple editions demonstrate how important the work is considered in the field. Also, an author may have written an important work 50 years ago that still has a strong influence on your field of study today. The background or reputation of the author is a good indicator. Through reading and class discussions you will become familiar with the influential (positive or negative) people in your discipline.

Knowing where an author is from or where a book is published indicates the state of argument in that particular country. It may be different from or similar to the discussions relevant to Australia. An important exercise is to make comparisons: think about areas where the discussions differ from or are similar to what you have read about Australia or your own country.

STRATEGIES FOR READING

At tertiary level, reading is done for a number of different objectives and each objective may involve a different reading strategy. Knowing why the reading is being done will help you to work out your strategies. Will you read a text to:

- prepare for a class?
- research for an assignment?
- go through material for an exam?

Skim reading or scanning

Scanning describes the quick type of reading that is done in order to pick up the general idea of a text. This is done by quickly skimming or scanning the passage for key words. The eye movement is very fast, as if being pushed along the page to take a quick X-ray of the important elements and blacking out anything minor. A technique used for skim reading is to quickly run a finger under the line you are reading so that you pick out only the key words. During skim reading you need to stay focused on getting the information, so you need to think about the content as you scan it. Thinking and scanning quickly means you need to *concentrate*.

You may not be used to skim reading. In your previous studies a close reading of material in order to memorise it may have been more relevant. However, at tertiary level studies in Australia, you will not have time to do such in-depth reading all of the time. Instead, by skim reading you will be able to pick up key ideas and then make a choice about what to do with the information. You may skim read to find the answers to a tutorial discussion paper or bits of information to help with an essay. You might then choose to change to a closer reading of the text and perhaps print out, photocopy or take notes from a section. As you practise, skimming (or scanning) will become a familiar skill and you will not feel like you are missing out on important information.

In-depth reading

In-depth reading takes more time than skim reading and is aimed at getting a detailed understanding of major ideas and how each section fits together in an argument. While you are doing this type of reading you are not looking for quick answers, but are using the information to develop your understanding of an issue and how it correlates with what has been presented in your classes and other reading you have done (critical thinking).

While you are reading, follow the line of the argument to see how a researcher or writer comes to a conclusion. Questions that will help you think critically about an argument are outlined in the box below.

> **READING AND CRITICAL THINKING**
>
> * Why has the author written this text?
> * What is the main idea or argument presented?
> * Is this idea different from or similar to others? How?
> * What sort of evidence is presented to justify the author's argument?
> * Is the evidence well researched?
> * Which points are not covered by the author that you think are important?

USING THE DICTIONARY

It is tempting to look up new words in the dictionary as you come across them in your reading. Checking for meaning is a good way to build up your own vocabulary, but you need to use the dictionary wisely.

The most obvious problem is frequent stopping to look up words. This can distract you from the general idea of the text, can be frustrating and, overall, a time-wasting exercise. It is often better to read to get a sense of the main idea, rather than concentrate on understanding each particular word. If an unfamiliar word actually hinders you from grasping the meaning, it may be necessary to use your dictionary.

Another problem occurs when the dictionary provides a few alternatives to an unfamiliar word but the original word is used in a way that is relevant only in a certain context, or to a specific field of study. For instance, according to the *Oxford Advanced Learner's Dictionary* (1989), *to fossilise* means:

1. (cause something) to become fossil: *fossilised leaves*;
2. (fig.) make (s'th) or become out of date or fixed: *old-fashioned fossilised attitudes*.

However, *fossilisation* in language studies refers to errors commonly made by the second-language learner that become bad language habits over a period of time. Thus, you should be aware that not all words listed in the dictionary necessarily match the meaning of the word in the context of the reading material. You may need to consult a more detailed dictionary that gives you examples of how to use the word in phrases and sayings (see *Useful references*), or check with a friend or teacher as to meanings.

If English is not your first language, you should still try to use a good English dictionary rather than rely on a direct translation-type dictionary, as a translation dictionary can be limiting and sometimes misleading. Also, the dictionary word may not give a full explanation. Most disciplines have specific dictionaries that list jargon and terms. Check with your lecturer if one is recommended for your course.

Many word-processing programs contain a spell check and thesaurus. Both are useful, if limited, tools. Make sure the program is set for Australian spelling. Also check your writing after the spell check, as this check does not distinguish all errors (e.g. *there* instead of *their*) and will not recognise some derivations of words. The thesaurus may be limited, and will not give you a sense of the context in which the words or phrases are used. If you are aware of these pitfalls you can use these functions wisely.

CONCLUSION

During your studies, reading and developing your vocabulary will be activities that take a lot of time and effort. Mastering skim reading and in-depth reading skills will take practice, particularly in staying focused. However, these techniques and critical thinking skills will help you make good use of your reading time.

6

Developing writing skills

Students are often confused or unclear about what is expected of them in preparing and presenting written assignments. Writing reports, essays, case studies and other documents may require accessing a lot more information than they may be used to from previous studies, or may involve different presentation methods. You may be asked to prepare a written assignment on an argument you know little about, or you may have to support an argument you do not really believe in. Often there are no right or wrong answers—it is purely a case of being able to present an argument and support it.

Assignments are one way of entering in the world of academic discourse. Your lecturers will evaluate how well you can present a logical, coherent and researched argument—an argument in which your point of view is clear. A lot of thought and *planning* is involved in *good* writing. This chapter will assist you to gain a clear idea of what is involved in writing and how to develop your understanding and skills in this area.

PREPARING THE ASSIGNMENT

Your own writing style

An important point to remember is that everyone approaches the writing process differently. Some plan thoroughly and write down every word, stopping to correct mistakes and check that all is going according to plan. Others write down ideas freely and do not make any corrections until they have finished. Some people are able to draft straight onto the word processor, while others use pen and paper. Any technique is fine as long as you are comfortable with your own writing and *revise* carefully. Having a clear plan set out beforehand helps guide the writing process. You will have your own way of expressing ideas, favourite terms or phrases. As you practise writing you will discover that there is a lot of scope to further develop your own writing style.

Audience

Assignments are written for a particular *audience*, often your lecturer. Before you start on the assignment, you should know to whom it is addressed. A specific audience may be stipulated by your lecturer. For example, if you were writing a marketing plan, your audience would be the board of directors in a work situation; if you were writing a journalistic piece, you would have to write for a particular group of magazine or newspaper readers.

Dealing with the topic

Analysing the topic or question is an integral part of preparing the assignment. Consider the key words and the instructions so that you do not waste time working hard on an assignment that does not really answer the question. Also, think about key words, required reading and argument structure. Underline the key words and circle the instruction words. What is the instruction word asking you to do: are you expected to compare, describe, analyse? (See appendix 4 for a list of commonly used instruction words.)

Once you are clear about the instructions, write each of the key words on a separate page of your notebook. Under each of the key words, jot down (write) any phrases, words or quotes that come to mind; this is called *brainstorming*.

Sometimes you are asked to choose a topic from a list or from personal interest. Beware of what seems, at first glance, to be the easiest—it is not always so. If you do choose your own topic, do some reading in the area and discuss the topic you are thinking about tackling with your lecturer to gain a better idea of its appropriateness. This will help avoid problems of diverging from the focus of the topic or pursuing a topic that may be interesting but too broad for the word limit.

Keep the question very clear in your mind so that you will be able to select appropriate reading for your note-taking. Think about the relevance of what you are reading as you go through the material—this will keep you on track and ensure that you do not take a lot of useless notes.

Reading to prepare an assignment

At tertiary level you are expected to read the relevant literature (books, journal articles, online texts), which will assist you in thinking about your topic and presenting it in the context of relevant issues. As you go on to higher-level studies the amount of research you are required to do will grow dramatically.

Your lecturer will give you a reading list that will help you start, and may give you some suggestions about the topic. Your class notes will also help start you off. However, you probably need to access further materials. When selecting reading material, you should look at those published, generally, in the past six years, as these will detail the most recent information relating to the topic. However, you will also need to look at any important, authoritative texts on the topic: for instance, an essay in the field of psychology may refer to the arguments of Freud (see chapter 5).

> *Study tip* *When selecting appropriate reading material, jot down key words and phrases relevant to your topic, and scan content pages and indexes for appropriate reading material.*

Thesis statement

Having done the reading and critical thinking, you will be ready to write a short statement about the topic. This is the *thesis statement* or *thesis argument*. The thesis statement explains your view clearly and is outlined in the introduction.

Planning the assignment

The next step is working out your outline or plan. Decide what your major points will be and write these at the top of a page in your notebook. Underneath, you will be able to organise some of the points you have come up with as part of your brainstorming and notes taken from your classes and reading.

In this outline, points should be ordered in a logical way so that the development of the argument is clear. Each main

---

PREPARING YOUR ASSIGNMENT

1 Write out the question.

2 Write down any key words, phrases and jargon in the question so that you can analyse what the question means.

3 Brainstorm issues focused on the topic.

4 Do your reading and note-taking (critical thinking!).

5 Decide on your point of view or argument.

6 Using separate sheets of paper, write down the main argument of each paragraph (at the top of the page).

7 Go back and jot down your supporting arguments for each paragraph.

8 Add relevant information from the literature to the appropriate planning pages. Do not forget to cite the references each time.

idea should appear with the supporting arguments slotted in underneath, adding relevant information from your reading.

WRITING THE ASSIGNMENT

The introduction

The introduction should explain your viewpoint clearly and how you will develop the argument—that is, outline the structure of the argument for the reader. A good strategy is to capture the reader's attention by explaining the importance or relevance of the topic in the context of the discipline. If you are going to focus on a particular aspect you need to explain this and why. For instance, if your question involves comparing banking practices in Asia and Australia, you may want to limit this to the past 15 years, and then explain why this is appropriate, perhaps arguing that it is only in recent years that comparative banking systems have been developed in certain countries and that previously other systems were in place.

The body

The body of the essay contains issues to support your main argument. The argument is structured in a linear way: each issue is presented with supporting evidence. Research is also used in the body of the essay to support each main point. One way to ensure that the essay is structured in a linear way is to provide headings for each section. The reader can then see the logical progression of the argument. At the end of each section a sentence should be inserted that ties the next section to what has just been presented. A useful tool in writing the body is the *paragraph*.

Paragraphing

Each paragraph contains a main idea or aspect of a main idea. Remember: one idea equals one paragraph. Students sometimes make the mistake of trying to crowd too many ideas into one paragraph but this just ends up confusing the reader.

The main idea of a paragraph is set out in the *topic sentence.* It specifies which issue will be dealt with in that paragraph. Most of the time, the topic sentence appears at the beginning of the paragraph but, depending on your style, it can appear in the middle or at the end. Not all paragraphs introduce a new issue but they may introduce a new aspect of the same issue. As you practise writing essays, it will become easier to

Figure 6.1   Structure of a paragraph

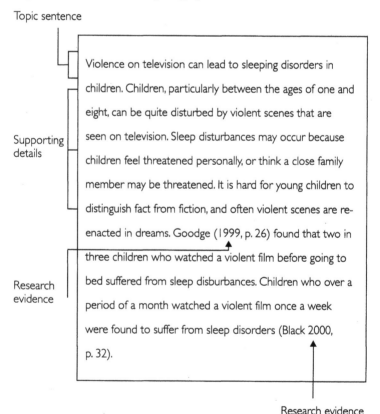

Topic sentence

Supporting details

Violence on television can lead to sleeping disorders in children. Children, particularly between the ages of one and eight, can be quite disturbed by violent scenes that are seen on television. Sleep disturbances may occur because children feel threatened personally, or think a close family member may be threatened. It is hard for young children to distinguish fact from fiction, and often violent scenes are re-enacted in dreams. Goodge (1999, p. 26) found that two in

Research evidence

three children who watched a violent film before going to bed suffered from sleep disburbances. Children who over a period of a month watched a violent film once a week were found to suffer from sleep disorders (Black 2000, p. 32).

Research evidence

write clear topic sentences. One good way of practising identifying topic sentences is to read a newspaper or journal article. Pick out a paragraph and find the sentence that presents (summarises) the idea in that section of writing. Sometimes you will find that the topic sentence is unclear or that the writer has two topic sentences in the one paragraph.

The length of a paragraph depends on the idea; there are no word rules. Some paragraphs will be four or five sentences in length, while others can be 20. The content and your own writing style will dictate this. As long as the main idea and supporting details are presented clearly (see Figure 6.1) there is no reason to worry about paragraph length, so be wary of formulaic advice. Writing is not maths.

The conclusion

The conclusion is the final paragraph, which brings together all the main points of the essay that support the thesis statement. No new ideas are presented in this paragraph. A lot of students write this last paragraph too quickly and without much thought as they are tired from the whole writing experience. However, it is important to *make an impact* here and lead the reader back over the main argument of the essay, then leave the reader with something to think about.

ESSAY WRITING

Good essay writing is a process requiring a number of strategies and can rarely be done well the night before the essay is due. The writing process is affected by your own writing style and the way you were taught to write according to cultural conventions. The discussions so far on working with the topic and planning all relate to preparing for essay writing.

Figure 6.2 is an example of an essay plan, and illustrates how the

Figure 6.2 Sample essay plan

Topic: *Is migration a problem in Australia?* ⟨ Discuss ⟩ (1500/2000 word essay)

Introduction

Thesis statement: <u>Benefits</u> far <u>outweigh negative aspects</u>, thus migration is a <u>positive</u> for <u>Australia</u>.

Body

1. Background

1a. Brief history of migration —rationale (Bird 1995),

                                       —white Australia policy (Mac 1966; Sim 1995),

                                       —multiculturalism (Ngyuen 1996);

1b. characteristics of migrants to Australia today—skilled migrants/refugees/ family reunion (Australian Bureau of Statistics 1997; BIPR 1996).

2. Benefits

2a. Skills brought in by migrants—business, craft, language, also willingness to do unskilled jobs (Bob 1995; Ting 1998; Brown 1996);

2b. population growth otherwise 0% without migration (ABS 1997);

2c. facilitating commercial industry, e.g. need for housing/manufacturing of goods, servicing of goods (Prom 1996; Wui 1998);

2d. encouraging tourism (Brown 1997);

2e. creating business links between Australia and migrants' home contacts (ABS 1997; Wui 1998);

2f. fostering multiculturalism (Deline 1998; French 1997).

3. Negative aspects

3a. Initial problems of settlement—unemployment, upgrade of language skills, health care etc. (Neid & Varag 1996, pp. 6–7);

3b. additional stress on environment (Blake 1999; James 1997);

3c. identity crisis (Ricmon 1969).

Conclusion

• All in all, migration positive for Australia.

• Careful environmental and social planning needed to ensure that negative issues are controlled and eliminated.

• Enrichment of country.

writer prepared her essay. The key words are underlined, while the instruction word is circled. The thesis statement is clear and explains the writer's opinion. The main and supporting arguments and evidence from research are all outlined. She has sequenced the issues. The planning of the conclusion is also evident.

Proofing/editing versus revising

A common error that students make is confusing the proofing or editing stage with the revising stage. Another is to try to do both at the same time.

Revising or *drafting* a piece of work is an important part of the creative process. The longer or more difficult the piece of work, the harder it is to maintain a clear argument, so revision needs to be done carefully. As you become more experienced, the revision process becomes more natural. Sometimes it is hard to delete a piece that has taken a long time to write but it may be necessary. You need to develop critical revision skills to help you refine your writing.

As a tertiary student, you must to be prepared to write drafts. One draft will not necessarily mean that you have written your best work. During the first stage of the drafting process the points in your outline will be turned into rough paragraphs. You will be writing to get the information down on paper. If you have time, it is helpful to put the draft in your folder for a couple of days before you return to it for redrafting. This will give you some distance from your writing, which is an essential element of the writing process. When you return to your writing, you need to check that the arguments are presented logically, that important points are clear and that supporting arguments are evident. You may need to redraft your essay a number of times before you are satisfied. Your first draft will mean writing so that all the ideas flow onto the page or screen. In your second draft you might check that there is only one issue discussed in each paragraph and that each sentence has one clear idea. During this stage you will probably refine the argument.

The *proofing* or *editing* stage is the last before you submit your paper. Proofing involves checking for typing errors, spelling, grammar, reference omissions, punctuation and presentation aspects. A checklist for both revising and proofing appears at the end of this chapter to guide you in the two processes.

> ### Some revision tips
>
> **Paragraphing** *Each paragraph should include one idea. Summarise that one idea in two or three words in the margin. This way you will be able to see clearly if you have too many ideas in that paragraph.*
>
> **Linearity** *By summarising the main idea of each paragraph in the margin, you can also check the linear logic of each idea. You may rearrange paragraphs to help outline the argument in a more logical and clearer manner.*
>
> **Distancing yourself** *Reading the text out aloud is one way of getting a sense of distance from what you have written. Read it critically, as if you were the lecturer—that is, not reading what you think it should say but what it actually says. Another strategy is writing the text, leaving it for a few days and then reading it again. Distancing yourself from your work before you check it is essential.*

Cultural differences

The essays you are required to write at tertiary level will be different from those you have written at high school. More research evidence and higher word limits may be required, and you need to deal with new and more demanding arguments. In addition, the way an argument is presented in Australia may be different from the way you would have presented it to a lecturer from your country.

According to English writing convention, major points are presented at the beginning of a paragraph while minor points are placed towards the end so that the most important point makes a stronger impact and is not lost in the overall message of the paragraph.

Kaplan[1] undertook a now-famous study in which essay structures of 600 samples were compared. He looked at some essays written by Arabic, Asian, Southern European and Russian students, and compared the writing styles with English writing conventions. Even though the results are based on generalised perceptions, they are helpful in explaining that, not only are there different grammar rules according to each language which make it difficult when writing in a second language, but different cultures have different ways of expressing ideas in writing. Construction of sentences and paragraphs reflects these differences. A general description of the findings is presented below and includes some sample texts taken from student work. These texts act as general guides which assist in illustrating how cultural differences may affect writing style.

Arabic

According to Arabic writing convention, writing is based on a series of parallel sentence constructions—that is, sentences which repeat what has just been stated, adding to or contradicting the idea. Also, the written text appears to be very descriptive compared with what is considered acceptable in English texts. In Figure 6.3 these aspects can be noted.

While the use of such structures are acceptable in Arabic written text, they are strange to English written conventions. The heavy use of descriptive phrases and parallelism would not be seen as appropriate in English texts: it would be regarded as

---

1. R.B. Kaplan, 'Cultural thought patterns in inter-cultural education', *Language Learning*, vol. 16, nos 3&4, 1966, pp. 1–20.

Figure 6.3   Sample of Arabic writing convention

> **Culture shock**
>
> Culture shock is a common characteristic for a newcomer to a country, and those who have never been to a country before may find it difficult and isolating. Because culture shock is isolating one feels strange. Feelings of loss of control, confusion, apprehension are common feelings. One may walk with new friends but feel a stranger among them. One may talk to acquaintances but feel an emptiness of soul. One may walk in the sun but feel that the way is dark. However, after a period of time an openness of feeling is discovered, then confusion becomes sense, apprehension becomes curiosity, loss of control becomes a sense of adventure.

Left annotations: Restating what a newcomer is (parallelism) · Descriptive language · The second part of the sentence negates the first (parallelism)

Right annotations: Adding to what has been stated already (parallelism) · The sentences have a lot of connectives to link the descriptions

repetitive or too poetic. Such phrases may remind the reader of the sort of sentence constructions found in the Bible.

Asian

In some Asian cultures, writers approach a topic in an indirect manner so that, to a native English speaker, they seem to be circling the topic without making a direct approach. Figure 6.4

Figure 6.4   Sample of Asian writing convention

> **What is culture shock?**
>
> Everyone belongs to a group of people by nationality, religion or both. One may enter lots of cultural groups and experience lots of cultures with modern-day travel and technology. Travelling is a good thing even though it may be difficult at the time. It may be only when one returns home that an appreciation for a foreign culture is discovered and a new sense of culture shock may occur. It seems odd in one's homeland but it is possible.

is an example. The example shows the writer circling around the topic of culture shock and, while alluding to it, not really answering the question clearly for the reader. My students tell me that the text is structured this way so as not to insult the intelligence of the reader (particularly a teacher, who already knows the answer to the question posed), while alluding to the answer to demonstrate that the writer also knows the answer.

Russian and Southern European

These writing conventions (such as French and Italian) tend to be more flexible than in English in that they permit digressions from the central argument. English writing conventions do not allow this and the writing would be labelled with comments like 'irrelevant' or 'what is the point of this section?'. Figure 6.5 is an example.

Figure 6.5   Sample of Russian and Southern European writing convention

Culture shock

Culture shock is a common characteristic for newcomers to a country. It can happen — Topic sentence

any time during the period a visitor stays in a country and can be mild or severe. Sometimes feelings of isolation, confusion, apprehension and even loss of control appear. *It seems strange that travel agents*

Digression to another issue → *don't provide information on this feeling. Perhaps they would rather avoid negative aspects, as they are a business making money.* However, after a period of time an openness of feeling usually takes over and a sense of adventure and curiosity negates any negatives feelings. Then one is free to enjoy the new curiosities in a new land—a land that is unexplored. *Each person is a Captain Cook discovering the delights of a foreign land to report to friends and families*

Digression to another issue → *left at home, who await eagerly the return of the son or daughter or friend, who has departed many months ago with many tears and will return to happy faces and, again, will experience many tears.*

While the digression in Figure 6.5 includes an interesting point regarding information available from travel agents, it is an additional idea that is not considered to be contributing to the topic sentence (regarding culture shock as a common experience of travellers) according to English writing traditions.

PRESENTING RESEARCH IN THE ASSIGNMENT

Presenting research in an assignment is all about analysing the interesting points you have discovered. You might find this strange at first if you have never been required to do it as part of your previous study experiences, but it is important to learn this. It is not sufficient simply to list a number of authors and their general arguments without any comments about how the literature adds to the topic being presented. Note the examples below.

Example 1

Andrews (1985) and Rose (1984) both discuss writer's anxiety.

Example 2

Andrews (1985) argues that writer's anxiety affects a person's self image and confidence as a writer. Rose (1984) argues that such anxiety can manifest itself ultimately as an obstacle to writing termed 'writer's block'. While Andrews (1985) and Rose (1984) present convincing research findings that demonstrate the emotional stress and poor attitude of those suffering from writer's anxiety, they do not provide any conclusive evidence as to the cause for such anxiety.

Critically analysing the literature involves noting particularly interesting points of an author's work. Sometimes this means pointing out what you perceive as negative, which is acceptable and appropriate in an Australian tertiary environment.

A trap that some students fall into is that they include a lot of information from research sources but not their own perspective. This demonstrates a general literature search but not the *student's* ability to analyse the literature critically from their perspectives, views and experience. The objective is to link the literature as *supporting* material for the main arguments.

The next step is to reference the source correctly. Your lecturer will inform the class of the referencing convention you should use (chapter 8 will help you with this). As you come across useful sources, record these in a separate notebook, your computer file or on an index card.

Quoting from sources

What is a quote?

A quote is a section of text made up of one word or a number of lines which are taken from another source. There are two types of quotations: *direct quotations*, where a text is copied exactly as it appears in the original; and *indirect quotations*, where text is presented as paraphrased or summarised information, in your own words. Remember that as soon as you draw on the work of someone else, either directly or indirectly, you must cite the source, otherwise it is *plagiarism*.

Why use quotations?

Quotations may be used to assist in your argument: they do not replace your own work but you can use other sources to illustrate, clarify and support your argument. This demonstrates that you have read and understood the arguments by the authorities in the field and can enter into discussion with other authorities. For instance, you may want to use other sources to demonstrate how an idea or method has been developed, or to refer to other studies that support your own, or compare the differences in the literature. You can use other sources to demonstrate that there are similarities between your perspective on a topic and that of a scholar, or to identify the differences between your research results and those of other scholars.

Direct quotations

Quoting directly refers to copying the exact words of another source. As soon as you use any of the author's words you must use quotation marks (' ... '). *Direct quotations* always need to be acknowledged or referenced. Short quotes can be inserted in the text:

> Ventura (1998, p. 86) states that it is valuable 'in developing cognitive linguistic skills'.

Quotes of three lines or more should be indented:

> In an innovative study, Ventura (1998, p. 86) states that:
>> Bilingualism is always seen as a great advantage in developing cognitive linguistic skills. There are no real problems of confusing languages by a bilingual child—often the child finds fun ways to work with the languages known.

Indirect quotations

Indirect quotations refer to ideas from other sources that you have presented in your own words. These need to be referenced carefully also. When you are referring to a particular idea presented on a page or in a section of a book, you need to add page numbers to the reference. There is no need for a page reference when there is an indirect quote that refers to a general idea discussed in the whole text. Indirect quotations appear in the text—for example:

> Bilingualism is seen as a positive learning process. In fact, Ventura (1998, p. 86) found that children enjoy dealing with a number of languages and confusion is not a problematic aspect.

The following are some useful phrases to use when paraphrasing:

- Pinas explains . . .
- As explained by . . .
- De Winton reports . . .

- As reported by . . .
- James indicates . . .
- Gillard points out . . .
- Hird observes . . .
- According to . . .
- As suggested by . . .
- Ward demonstrates . . .
- In a study by . . .
- Morris theorises . . .
- Research undertaken by Pedro indicates tha
- Lynch notes . . .
- Farrell defines . . . as . . .
- As discussed in Pinas and Hynh . . .

How many quotes should I use?

There is no standard answer. Select quotes tha
tant role in the presentation of *your* argument
much of a quote as is necessary. Too many qu
direct) can overpower your ideas, so that the
up looking like a list of everyone else's theories.
tertiary environment, it is essential that an assi
the view of the writer, and that is you. Even
with other scholars, you need to explain why.

> **Study tip** *Always try to find the original so*
> *mation you are citing. If this is not possible,*
> *source.*

Adapting quotes

You may adapt quotes to suit the text if, for ins
mar does not suit the rest of your writing
wording flow. Compare the following.

Original:

> 'Firstly it is vital to critically analyse each word for definition, then proceed to break down the question so that it can be considered fully.' De Winton (1998, p. 7)

Adapted quote:

> De Winton (1998, p. 7) suggests 'critically analys[ing] ... [the] word[ing] for definition, then proceed[ing] to break down the question so that it can be considered fully'.

Changes made to the original quote can be demonstrated using square brackets '[ ]' or an ellipsis ' ... ' for changes to original word endings, or for additional words inserted so that the quote makes sense. Alterations should be made so that the text makes sense, without changing the original meaning of the quote (see appendix 5 for a list of common punctuation marks).

WRITING STYLE

Dealing with new vocabulary

As part of your reading and classes you will come across new vocabulary, terms and phrases. A quick check of new words can be made using your dictionary (as discussed in chapter 5). However, when writing you may want to express an idea and not be able to think of the appropriate word or term. A thesaurus is often more helpful than a dictionary in such a case, as it contains lists of synonyms (similar words and phrases) and antonyms (word of opposite meaning). These lists are sometimes organised under topics. In *Roget's Thesaurus*, you need to go to the index-type list at the back, look up a word that is approximate to what you want to say and then look up the page number given. For instance, if you have the word 'reason' but are looking for something else, you may come up with 'motive', 'rationale', 'intention' or 'objective', among many others.

Using connectives

Connectives (or conjunctions) are used between sentences or paragraphs to link ideas and help the argument flow to make it interesting and easy for the reader to follow the argument. Appendix 6 is a list of connectives, each expressing different functions. Using connectives makes the writing interesting, although having too many can be a strain to read.

> ### Some tips on writing style
>
> **Complicated phrases** *If what you want to say seems complicated and you end up with long, awkward sentences, try some short, clear sentences. Avoid vocabulary you are unsure of. Check to see how words are used in sentences before using them yourself.*
>
> **Use of headings** *Separating the text of the study with the use of short, interesting titles is a good way to keep the work organised as you write and the reader focused.*
>
> **Jargon** *Try to avoid the excessive use of jargon. Sometimes it is hard to omit altogether because a certain field of study depends on it, but use it only when unavoidable and make sure you understand the meaning.*

Using non-discriminatory language

There has been a strong move towards avoiding discriminatory language in communication, in order to encourage equal rather than power-based relationships. This reflects the concern in general society for developing equitable practices.

One of the commonest aspects of non-discriminatory language is gender-free language. Consider the following sentences:

a. Man is constantly striving to better his living condition.
b. A student should always get to know the library facilities. He should book a library tour and spend time using the catalogue.

   c. A doctor is a highly respected member of society. He is often
      called on to be more of a counsellor than a medical practitioner.

All the above examples ignore the role of women and thus are
considered to be discriminatory. It takes a bit of rethinking in
English to come up with appropriate alternatives, as there is no
neutral pronoun to refer to a person (as there is in some languages). Other strategies must be employed in English such as
the use of alternative words, the 'he/she' construction or the
plural form of the noun instead of the singular. The above examples have been rewritten to eliminate any discrimination:

   a. Humanity is constantly striving to better living conditions.
      'Man' is substituted by the general noun 'humanity' and the pronoun
      'his' is omitted.

   b. A student should always get to know the library facilities. He or
      she should book a library tour and spend time using the
      catalogue.
      'He' is retained while the pronoun 'she' is added. Sometimes you
      will see 'he/she'. Note that this strategy works for the odd sentence,
      although an essay full of the term 'he and she' is laborious to read
      and hinders style.

   c. Doctors are highly respected members of society. They are often
      called on to be counsellors more than medical practitioners.
      The plural form of the noun 'doctor' is used instead of the singular.

The same sort of care needs to be taken in avoiding racist or
other forms of discriminatory language.

Adopting an academic tone

There are certain conventions regarding written academic discourse which differ from general spoken communication. Your
tone in an essay should be more formal than, say, when discussing issues in your tutorial. While there is a move towards
using plain English and getting rid of jargon, written communication is ruled by certain formal conventions. Reading journal

articles and texts in your discipline will help you get a general idea of the sort of tone to adopt, though no-one expects you to write according to 'publication standards'.

As you become more familiar with academic-style writing you will learn to use supporting arguments in the way you organise a paper to make your views clear. Statements to avoid are 'I think', 'In my opinion', 'I know that . . .'. Once you have sorted out your supporting evidence, you need to present it using an academic tone. Try phrases such as 'It seems that . . .', 'The evidence tends to demonstrate that . . .', 'Studies suggest that . . .'.

Avoid idioms and slang. While these are acceptable in general conversation, they are usually inappropriate in a written assignment. If there are good reasons why an idiomatic phrase should be used, this should be inserted in quotation marks: for instance, if you are quoting a subject in your report regarding the presentation of politicians on television, you might say that there is a feeling that *some politicians are just 'talking heads'*. If you wanted to avoid the idiom 'talking heads', you could say that *some politicians appear to be reiterating lines on behalf of someone else rather than explaining personal views.*

Sometimes having too many points or explanations means that your sentence is too long and complex. Try breaking up the explanation into a few short, clear sentences. Get the message down on paper. Once you have a clear piece of communication, you can work on linking sentences using connectives or reviewing vocabulary.

PRESENTING THE ASSIGNMENT

The presentation of an assignment is an important aspect of academic work. Poor presentation can result in poor marks. Some departments or lecturers stipulate particular presentation styles. The following is a guide, but check to see what the requirements are for your courses.

- *Page.* Use one side of the page only and number pages carefully. Note that reports entail specific numbering methods.

- *Acronyms.* It is appropriate to use acronyms of commonly known organisations. However, the first time one is mentioned in the assignment the title should be written out *in full* followed by the initials in brackets—for example:

  the Federal Trade Commission (FTC) often publishes . . .

- *Language.* Your assignments should be presented using clear, precise language. It is true that at an educational institution a certain level of formality is expected but avoid using lots of formal-sounding words as the message may get lost. Also avoid using slang, idioms and clichés. Through practice, you will develop your own writing style. You will learn to develop a certain distance from your topic so that it is presented in an objective, rather than emotional manner: for instance, it is best to avoid terms such as 'I think'.

- *Title page.* A title page should be inserted as the cover page of each assignment. This should include the topic or question, student name, course or unit of work, lecturer's name and date of submission.

- *Word processing.* Most lecturers ask for assignments to be typed out. If this is difficult, write it out clearly and legibly, or you may have the assignment returned and a resubmission requested.

- *Margins.* A 15 mm margin on each side of the page is generally requested so that lecturers have enough space to write in any comments. If it is going to be bound, take this into account when calculating your margins.

- *Font.* A 12 point (pt) clear font is acceptable. If the writing is too small, the lecturer may have trouble reading it. Headings are usually in 14 pt or 16 pt, and appear in bold. Ensure that headings are presented in a consistent manner (i.e. font size and style).

- *Copies.* It is a good idea to keep a hard copy of your assignment in case the original is lost or destroyed accidentally. Do not rely on a copy on your disk.

- *Abbreviations.* Do not use abbreviations such as & or *etc.* except in tables, figures and text in parentheses. Instead, use the full phrase: for & use *and*; for *etc.* use *and so on* or *for instance.*

What is your lecturer looking for?

As explained, each task that is undertaken demonstrates your general progress in developing academic competence. Good assignments will demonstrate that you:

- have read and understand the literature in your field of studies;
- are able to construct and present *your* argument;
- can present an assignment according to written conventions (i.e. with references, bibliography, appendix etc.);
- are able to draw on sources in your field in presenting your argument;
- are able to use the key words and jargon in your field;
- are able to present a written text which is free of proofreading errors;
- are able to submit a professionally presented written text.

REVIEWING THE ASSIGNMENT

Reread your written assignment once it has been returned to you. It is important that you read the lecturer's comments (feedback) and understand why these were made. If you do not understand a lecturer's comment, set a time to discuss the feedback. If there are only a few comments or only a mark is given, politely ask for more feedback to help you improve your next assignment. You may be able to discuss the assignment and the feedback, in a constructive way, with your study group or friends, to see what was done well and what needs to be improved.

WRITING SUMMARIES

A summary is a concise collection of the main points of text. It is a descriptive piece: that is, you are required only to describe what was presented, not interpret the arguments. The key to writing a good summary is the ability to pick out and clearly synthesise the main points. Use your own words and avoid quoting unless absolutely necessary; even then, use only a few words rather than a lengthy description. The summary should be presented with a brief introduction and conclusion and demonstrate the same good writing techniques that have been explained already.

CONCLUSION

As you proceed in your studies, you will get the opportunity to develop your own writing techniques, including planning, sequencing of main arguments and incorporating research as part of the development of the argument. Developing good writing skills will be a crucial part of your progress and careful planning and drafting are important elements in improving these skills.

✓ CHECKLIST FOR WRITTEN ASSIGNMENTS

Revising

☐ Are the ideas easy and clear to follow? If not, what changes should I make? Would examples help?

☐ Does the introduction clearly outline the argument?

☐ Are there any confusing parts I should rewrite?

☐ Does the conclusion clearly bring together the main ideas and finish in a strong way?

☐ Does each paragraph have one clear idea? (If not, the ideas may need separating and some rewriting.)

☐ Does the argument flow from one paragraph to another?

☐ Do the headings reflect what is in the paragraph below?

☐ Are the paragraphs in the correct order?

☐ Is there repetition? Which bit should I delete?

☐ Has the question been answered?

☐ Have all the main points been included?

☐ Are the supporting arguments clear?

☐ Are the quotations linked to the main arguments?

Proofing

☐ Are all the references cited?

☐ Are the references set out correctly?

☐ Is the spelling accurate?

☐ Is the grammar accurate?

☐ Is the punctuation accurate?

☐ Are all the appendixes included?

☐ Are the margins an appropriate size?

☐ Is the assignment double-spaced (if necessary)?

☐ Have you included words whose meaning you are not sure of? (If so, delete or substitute.)

☐ Is the bibliography set out correctly?

☐ Are the headings clear?

☐ Is the cover page included?

☐ Are the page numbers included?

☐ Is a spare copy filed away neatly?

☐ Is a list of tables/figures included?

☐ Are tables/figures numbered appropriately?

☐ Is a brief description of each table/figure included?

☐ Is there a back-up copy on disk prepared, labelled and stored away safely?

7

Report writing

A report is different from an essay in its format and the way it treats information. A report generally presents facts. As the report writer, you are putting forward an analysis of information or data. Depending on the discipline (such as business, health sciences, engineering) the information may be based largely on statistics. The aim of the report is to present facts from which conclusions can be drawn and recommendations made.

Depending on the discipline, a report will include a number of different sections (see box on the next page). Under each section there will be subsections, each of them numbered clearly.

STRUCTURE OF THE REPORT

Title page

The title page should include the topic, your name, the lecturer's name, the date of submission and the course or subject title.

A BUSINESS REPORT MIGHT INCLUDE	A SCIENTIFIC REPORT MIGHT INCLUDE
Title page	Title page
Table of contents	Table of contents
List of figures (if relevant)	List of figures (if relevant)
List of tables or illustrations (if relevant)	List of tables or illustrations (if relevant)
Executive summary	Abstract
Introduction	Introduction
Body	Body
Results	Methodology
Discussion	Results
Conclusion	Discussion
Recommendations (if relevant)	Conclusion
Reference list/endnotes (depending on the referencing system recommended)	Reference list/endnotes (depending on the referencing system recommended)
Appendixes	Appendixes

Table of contents

In this part you list the headings of sections and subsections of the report and their page numbers. It allows the reader to gain an overview of the parts of the report and how it is structured. Appendixes also appear, with a brief description of what they include. Roman numerals (i, ii, iii ...) indicate such pages as the title page, table of contents, list of figures and tables and the executive summary. The main body has arabic page numbers (1, 2, 3 etc.). Page numbering for appendixes runs on sequentially from the main body.

List of figures or tables

Under the heading (either List of figures or List of tables), list the number, explanation and the page number of each figure or table. The aim is to allow the reader to look up a particular figure/table easily without having to scan the whole report. Below is an example.

Executive summary or abstract

The summary should provide an overall view, or *synopsis*, of the report. Here, you should summarise the important points so that the reader has a clear idea of what the report discusses, its conclusions and recommendations, before the body of the report is even read. This section is usually no longer than a page.

Introduction

The introduction covers four aspects. First, the *aim* of the report, which explains why it has been written in terms of the relevance or importance of the topic and what you are trying to show through writing this report. Second, the *authorisation*, which details who the report is being written for. Third, the *methodology*, which explains briefly how you gathered the data or information (e.g. through the literature, interviews or questionnaires). Finally, the *limitations*, which is a statement of what has not been covered and why, so that the report has a clear framework. By the end of the introduction, the reader should be clear about the focus of the topic and know what to expect when reading the report.

Body of the report

The body of the report contains sections and subsections, each with numbered headings. It is important to have headings that catch the attention of the reader. The headings should be succinct and explain what is covered in each of the sections in this part of the document. They should be numbered sequentially and presented in a consistent style.

In the body, you need to present all the facts, any relevant background information with a bearing on the topic, any events and consequences. The information is presented in the same way as other sections, through concise, clear sentences. It is also common to use points set out as a list using bullets (•) to mark each point. Also, references should be made to any diagrammatical information that is included to illustrate a point.

Methodology

This section outlines the research design—that is, your sample, how you did the investigation and why you chose to use a particular method to investigate the subject. You should also detail the equipment you used to undertake your research. The methodology section has to be detailed enough for another person to follow the instructions and copy your steps. Thus, each step needs to be detailed sequentially. This section is usually subdivided into various headings, such as *Sample* and *Rationale*.

Results

In this section, the results of your research should be set out clearly—that is, a brief explanation of what you have found and whether these findings are significant. Tables and figures may be included to demonstrate your findings, particularly if these are statistically based. You do not need to evaluate the information here, that will be part of the next section, your discussion.

Discussion

This section allows you to analyse the information presented in the body of the report and show how it relates to the aims of the study. It is important not to bring in any new information here but to draw together your findings and how these are linked to the information you have already presented in the body. The significance of each of the findings and any interesting points are discussed in terms of why you think you obtained such findings. It is quite acceptable to talk about the possibility of errors or limitations of the study. This shows that you are thinking as a researcher.

Conclusion

This is a short section based on the discussion. Here you should draw together main points of interest from the data presented and the discussion of the data. Your opinion should be very clear here—that is, the main facts should be interpreted clearly for the reader.

Recommendations

As pointed out earlier, you need to make recommendations based on the information presented in the report. For instance, an accounting report on various stock control systems will make recommendations as to which system, or combination of systems, is appropriate in a given situation.

Reference list/endnotes

This section is a list of all the sources used in preparing the report. You need to find out which referencing system is used in your department. (See chapter 8.)

Appendixes

This section contains information that is useful to the study—for example, tables and figures from other reports. While the most important information is contained in the body of the report, any other useful material is included in the appendixes so as not to interrupt the flow of the main argument. This is particularly important if a report has many tables and figures, as too many in the body make the report difficult to read.

SETTING OUT FIGURES

Such items as diagrams, graphs and tables should be included only if relevant. Those figures that are very important to the argument should be included in the body, and secondary data should be included as an appendix. You need to *explain* what these figures indicate. If you obtain them from other sources, you must cite the original text and you may need to get permission to use them. Each figure should be numbered according to the section it is in, and appear with a brief explanation below it. Figure 7.1 is an example.

SETTING OUT TABLES

Every table should be numbered consecutively and followed by a brief explanation of what is represented. This explanation can be written in a slightly smaller font. Some lecturers prefer all tables and figures to appear as appendixes (in this case, each one is on a separate page). Others prefer the main data to appear in the body of text. Check with your lecturer.

CONCLUSION

A report is set out according to specific conventions, however, report writing involves the same good writing techniques already

Figure 7.1   Sample figure

This graph is the first in section 3 of the report   Brief heading

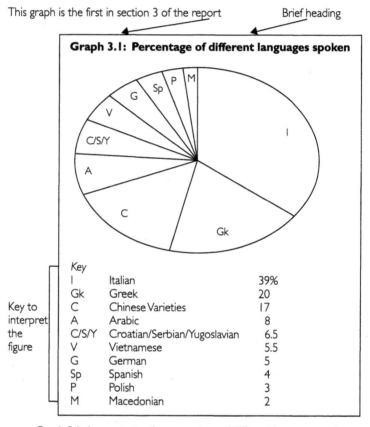

Graph 3.1 demonstrates the percentage of different languages spoken
in the state according to the 1993 census (Dept of Research 1995).

Brief explanation   Citation

discussed (in chapter 6). The different sections of a report are
included here as a guide. To gauge style and format, compare
these to other reports written specifically for your discipline.

8

Referencing

Referencing is an important component of academic discussion and is used to acknowledge sources. You should understand the purpose of referencing (citing) and how to reference different sources of information. There are two main systems for referencing: the *Harvard referencing system* and the *footnote/endnote system*, both commonly used conventions.

A full reference (citation) details a text's author, title, publication date, publisher and place published. From any textbook you can see that whenever an author draws on information from another source, that source is acknowledged in a reference so that the reader can access that work in order to follow a discussion on a particular issue. For example, a full reference for a *book* or *text* is set out as in Figure 8.1.

A full reference for a *journal article* may be set out as in Figure 8.2.

Figure 8.1 Sample book reference

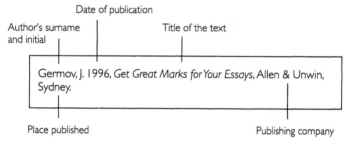

Figure 8.2 Sample journal article reference

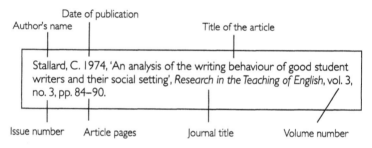

WHY USE REFERENCES?

As part of your studies you will access and read works by others in your field. Your lecturers will expect you to be familiar with the authorities in your discipline and to be able to present a critical argument that draws on the views of other scholars. These views may be introduced to support your argument, to present an opposing perspective or to represent a general feel for views on the topic on which you will present your ideas. Through presenting an argument that takes into account the views and research of scholars—whether in a tutorial, as a presentation or in a written assignment—you are entering into academic discourse.

Whenever you quote or use information from another source, you must acknowledge this source. Failure to acknowledge another person's work or ideas is a very serious matter and is known as plagiarism (see box below).

> Plagiarism occurs when a student tries to present someone else's ideas, information or results *as his/her own*; this is considered stealing and is very serious. A student may be asked to resubmit, or may fail an assignment. In extreme cases, he/she may incur a fine or even be dismissed from the institution.

WHICH REFERENCING SYSTEM TO USE?

Your lecturer or department will advise you of the referencing system recommended for your written assignments. You should become familiar with this system, as it is easy to confuse systems. When using a referencing system you are following rules or conventions. The guide below helps you with the most common aspects of referencing: the most important thing is to *be consistent* in your use of italics, punctuation and inclusion of details.

The Harvard referencing system

This system is also known as the *author/date system*. References are made in the body of the text and the full citation details appear in the bibliography or reference list. For example:

> 'Referencing correctly should not be overlooked when completing a written assignment. Often this stage is rushed at the end. Give yourself time to proofread your references, making sure all the sources you cite in your paper are also in your bibliography.' (De Winton 1998, p. 5)

Note that the name of the author is followed by the year of publication, followed by a comma and page reference. The page is referred to by the abbreviation 'p.'. Two or more pages are referred to by the abbreviation 'pp.'.

A *general reference* to an argument by a scholar can be noted as:

It is theorised (Wajcman 1994) that technology . . .

or

Wajcman (1994) theorises that technology . . .

When a *direct reference* is made to an author's argument, the author's name is mentioned in the text with the year; if appropriate, page details are included in brackets:

It has been suggested by Wajcman (1994, pp. 3–4) that technology is the most influential factor in recent social changes.

or if a general reference is made to a work:

Not all studies, such as that of Wajcman (1994), agree with . . .

Referring to a *journal article* follows a similar pattern, with the author's surname, date and page reference if applicable:

Stallard (1966, pp. 84–90) suggests . . .

The full citation in the bibliography or references list would appear as:

Stallard, C. 1974, 'An analysis of the writing behaviour of good student writers and their social setting', *Research in the Teaching of English*, vol. 3, no. 3, pp. 84–90.

Referring to several authors follows the same conventions—that is, the author's surname and the date of each writer's work in brackets; alternatively, you can list the authors in brackets separating each author's details with a semicolon:

Wright (1989), Rong (1994) and Nsure (1996) found that . . .

or

Results suggest that academics are unsure about the value of technology as a research tool (Wright 1989; Rong 1994; Nsure 1996).

Referring to more than one work by an author follows the same pattern. Works are set out chronologically according to the date of publication and separated by commas:

Jackson (1981, 1990, 1997) presents the results of his various studies . . .

Sometimes in a written assignment you will refer to *an author who has published several texts in one year*. In this case, letters of the alphabet are used to distinguish between the different works. The works are separated by a comma. The same alphabetical references are then used in the bibliography or reference list:

Vici (1998a, 1998b) has considered the question of . . .

When there are *two authors*, both names should be written out. If the names appear in brackets, then use the symbol & (ampersand) between the authors' names:

Dante and Pavarotti (1998) indicate . . .
(Dante & Pavarotti 1998)

If there are *three authors or more*, the citation includes the surname of the first author only followed by the Latin abbreviation *et al.* This demonstrates that there are other authors (however, all the authors' names should appear in the bibliography, just as they are listed on the title page of the original work):

Totto et al. (1998, p. 12) indicate . . .

Reference to *an author who appears in a text by another author* or editor follows the same pattern (using the abbreviation *ed.* for editor):

Glitz (1998) states . . .

and the full reference would appear as:

Glitz, E. 1998, 'Saturday Night Fever Syndrome', in *Social Rituals*, D. Ward (ed.), Beegee Publishing, Melbourne.

When an *organisation*'s name appears as the author of material you are referencing, this name is cited in place of the author. If the abbreviation is well known, this can be used in the body of your assignment (although the organisation's full name must be detailed in the bibliography):

As indicated by the AGPS (1994) . . .

and the full reference, with the edition used and clearly identified, would be:

Australian Government Publishing Service (AGPS) 1994, *Style Manual: For Authors, Editors and Printers*, 5th edn, AGPS, Canberra.

Citing government publications is similar to citing books. The author may be a government department or a committee; thus, this name is used as the author:

Department of Trade (1995) figures show . . .

References to articles in newspapers follow the same principle as those already outlined: that is, the name of the newspaper, the date, section (if applicable) and page:

The Australian (27 June 1997, p. A20) reported that . . .

If there is an *identifiable author*, the citation is the same as that for journals:

Winton (1997, p. 2) . . .

and the full reference would appear as:

Winton, D. 1997, 'Australian flora', *The Agricultural Weekly*, 8 January, p. 2.

The footnote/endnote system

This system is sometimes referred to as the Oxford system. Each quote or reference is numbered sequentially with the corresponding full reference written out. If the full references are inserted at the end of the page, these are called *footnotes*. If they appear in a list at the end of the chapter or assignment, they are called *endnotes*. Each reference appears in the order in which the work is mentioned in the text, and is listed with two lines between each full citation.

When word-processing your written assignment, the program you use may format the number automatically or you can select the *superscript* function under *font*. If this does not work, typing the number in brackets is acceptable.

Note that at least two line spaces should be left between the last line of the text and the first line of the footnote. The author's first name or initial appears before the surname, followed by a comma and the title, which is either written in italics or underlined. The page number appears at the end (figure 8.3).

Figure 8.3 Sample footnote

'Referencing correctly should not be overlooked when completing a written assignment. Often this is rushed at the end. Give yourself time to proofread your references making sure all the sources you cite in your paper are also in your bibliography.'[4]

The footnote that appears at the bottom of the page will look like this:

4. T. De Winton, *Studying at University*, Len Books, Geelong, 1998, p. 5.

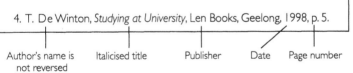

| Author's name is not reversed | Italicised title | Publisher | Date | Page number |

Mentioning the author in the text would also be indicated by a footnote:

It has been suggested by Wright[1] *that* . . .

or

It has been suggested[1] that . . .

The note to appear at the end of the page or as an endnote would be:

1. J. Wright, *Learning and Empowerment*, Hard Knocks University Press, Preston, 1989, pp. 23–24.

A *reference to a journal article* contains similar information, as well as volume and issue number. The article appears in quotation marks, while the title of the journal appears in italics:

V. Vici, 'French wines', *Harvest Magazine*, vol. 6, no. 4, 1996, pp. 13–22.

Referring to several authors at the same time is done by listing the surnames:

Wright[1], Rong[2] and Nsure[3] outline theories on learning.

Remember, the notes appear with space between each one:

1. J. Wright, *Learning and Empowerment*, Hard Knocks University Press, Preston, 1989.

2. P. Rong, *Introducing Learning*, Griffin Press, London, 1994.

3. S. Nsure, *Learning Research*, Park Press, Melbourne, 1997.

Two or more sequential references to a text can be demonstrated by using the full footnote the first time and then the Latin abbreviation *ibid.* to tell the reader to refer to the previous footnote for the full reference:

1. J. Wright, *Learning and Empowerment*, Hard Knocks University Press, Preston, 1989.

2. ibid., p. 4.

3. ibid., pp. 18–19.

Repeated references to a text that are not in sequential order can also be demonstrated by the Latin abbreviation *op. cit.* This abbreviation is preceded by the surname, so that the reader can refer to the author and page details directly:

1. J. Wright, *Learning and Empowerment*, Hard Knocks University Press, Preston, 1989, p. 62.

2. P. Rong, *Introducing Learning*, Griffin Press, London, 1994.

3. Wright, op. cit., p. 5.

Referring to more than one work by an author in one reference follows the same convention, with works set out chronologically according to the date of publication:

Various studies by Rong[1] demonstrate . . .

1. P. Rong, *Introducing Learning*, Griffin Press, London, 1994.
   P. Rong, *Memory and Learning*, Griffin Press, London, 1995.
   P. Rong, *Intellectuals and Intellect*, Griffin Press, London, 1998.

Sometimes, in your written assignment, you will refer to *an author who has published several texts in one year*. In this case, letters of the alphabet can be used to distinguish between the different works. Remember that the same alphabetical references are used in the bibliography or reference list:

Vici[2] has considered the question of . . .

and the full reference would appear as:

2. V. Vici, 'Vini italiani', *L'internazionale*, vol. 5, no. 1, 1996a, pp. 2–20.
   V. Vici, 'French wines', *Harvest Magazine*, vol. 6, no. 4, 1996b, pp. 13–22.

When an *organisation* is the author of material you want to reference, the name of the organisation is inserted as the author. When there is *more than one edition*, the exact one used is identified by the abbreviation *edn*:

Australian Government Publishing Service, *Style Manual: For Authors, Editors and Printers*, 5th edn, AGPS, Canberra, 1994.

References to articles in newspapers follow the same pattern. The name of the newspaper, the date, section (if applicable) and the page:

The Australian[1] reported that . . .

and the full reference would be:

> *The Australian*, 'Australia as a republic', 2 January 2000, p. 1.

When there is an *identifiable author*, the conventions are the same as those applying to journals:

> D. Winton, 'Australian flora', *The Agricultural Weekly*, 8 January 1997, p. 2.

Citing government publications is similar to citing books. When the author is a government department or a committee, this name is used as the author:

> Department of Trade, *A Guide to Australian Exports*, AGPS, Canberra, 1992.

ABBREVIATIONS COMMONLY USED IN REFERENCING			
edn	edition	et al.	and others
ed.	editor	vol./Vol.	volume
eds	editors	no./No.	number
p.	page	re/Re	regarding
pp.	pages	V	version
ibid.	in the same work	op. cit.	in the work already cited

REFERENCING ELECTRONIC SOURCES

The use of electronic sources of information in scholarly work is becoming more common. Such sources include the Internet, CD-ROM and e-mail. Referencing conventions are still being consolidated by the International Organisation for Standardisation, but the following can be used as a guide to standard usage.

Online sources

The conventions for online sources resemble those already discussed. The reference begins with the author, whenever possible. Usually the name can be found at the end of the page as an e-mail address. Sometimes you will find only nicknames (handles). If the real name cannot be found, use the handle as the author's details. The full date of publication of the work will usually appear at the end of a Web page or at the beginning of a commercial program. If there are no details of month or day, you can use the abbreviation 'n.d.' (no date) (e.g. *n.d./1998*).

The full title of the information should be written out as it appears in the original source (see Figure 8.4). This is followed by the type of document and then the full address so that the reader can access the work. The date you access the work should also be given (in brackets), as the work may be modified by the time a reader accesses the information, in which case it can be seen that you have accessed the page before modifications were made. This may also mean that the reader can access the information listed under the date you have recorded rather than a modified version.

Every Web address or URL (uniform resource locator) is followed by a space and the details needed to call up (retrieve) the online information. If a URL is longer than one line, then it is broken at a slash and continues to the second link. A URL has no punctuation mark at the end.

Journals and newspaper articles on the Internet

Journals and newspaper articles can now also be accessed electronically. The reference convention for these follows a similar pattern, including the author, date, title of the article, medium in which it appears and title of the journal or article. Next the volume number and issue number are detailed, as well as the page references. Do not forget to include the full address in the bibliography so that the reader can locate the information and, of course, the date you accessed the document:

Harvard referencing system

Gibili, D. 1997, 'Coalition crisis', *Online Journal of Pedantic Politics* [Online serial] vol. 6, no. 2, http://www.pedantpolis/coal~cris.html (Date accessed 12 August 1997).

Footnote system

1. D. Gibili, 'Coalition crisis', *Online Journal of Pedantic Politics*, 1997, vol. 6, no. 2. [Online serial], http://www. pedantpolis/ coal~cris.html (Date accessed 12 August 1997).

Figure 8.4 Samples of online references

Harvard referencing system

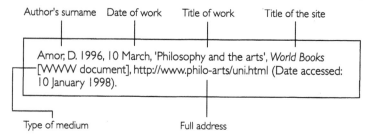

Footnote referencing system

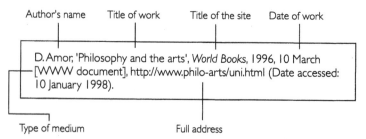

Citing CD-ROM information

Again, similar conventions are applicable. You start off with the author's name, the date, title of the article, name of the

CD-ROM, version (if applicable), identification of the medium, followed by the name of the publishing company:

Harvard referencing system
Simple, R. 1998, 'Jumping tricks', *Croft Adventures*, V. 2 [CD-ROM], Microhard Corporation.

Footnote referencing system
1. R. Simple, 'Jumping tricks', *Croft Adventures*, V. 2 [CD-ROM], Microhard Corporation, 1998.

Citing e-mail information

Referencing information from a *discussion list* sometimes occurs as part of your research-gathering process. The referencing details would look like this:

Harvard referencing system
Gibili, D. 10 May 1998, 'Defensive formations', *Football Tactics* [Online], footballlist@fans.lv.vs (Date accessed 11 May 1998).

Footnote referencing system
1. D. Gibili, 'Defensive formations', *Football Tactics*, 1998, 10 May [Online], footballlist@fans.lv.vs (Date accessed 11 May 1998).

Citing personal e-mail

This also carries with it certain conventions. As part of research-ing activities, you may have contact with a lecturer, author or authority via e-mail. This information may be useful to your research and you may want to draw on it:

Harvard referencing system
Gibili, D. (gibilid@newhaven.com.vs), 21 August 1998. Re: Defensive formations, e-mail to V. Vici (viciv@cold mail.com.vs).

Footnote referencing system
1. D. Gibili (gibilid@newhaven.com.vs). Re: Defensive formations, e-mail to V. Vici (viciv@coldmail.com.vs), 21 August 1998.

CREATING A REFERENCE LIST OR BIBLIOGRAPHY

Sometimes there is confusion over the difference between a reference list and a bibliography. A reference list outlines all the sources cited in the body of your written assignment, while a bibliography is an extended list which includes generally relevant sources that have been used in preparing the assignment but may not have been cited. The presentation of sources is the same for both reference list and bibliography.

How to present a reference list or bibliography

There are some conventions that dictate how a bibliography is presented. Citations are always presented in alphabetical order, according to the first author's surname. The second line of a citation is always indented to highlight the alphabetical order. Care should be taken with punctuation and also that the text is cited according to the original language used, particularly if dealing with foreign languages.

A lecturer may ask that texts, journals and electronic sources be separated. If this is the case, the same conventions apply as to presentation.

The details of how you present a reference list or bibliography also depend on the referencing system adopted for the body of the text. However, if you do use the footnote/endnote system, there is probably no need to attach a reference list or bibliography. It would be worthwhile checking on your lecturer's expectations for the assignment. If you are asked to present such a list or bibliography, the format is exactly the same as that outlined for the footnote/endnote referencing system, except that the surname is put in front of the initials to highlight the alphabetical order. Also, no page numbers are given except in the case of journal articles. These are only minor differences, so it is important not to get confused: *consistency* is important.

Harvard referencing system

The box below gives an example of a bibliography or referencing list according to the modified Harvard referencing system.

HARVARD REFERENCING SYSTEM

Australian Government Publishing Service 1994, *Style Manual: For Authors, Editors and Printers*, 5th edn, AGPS, Canberra.

Gibili, D. 1997, 'Coalition crisis', *Online Journal of Pedantic Politics* [Online serial] vol. 6, no. 2, http://www.pedantpolis/coal~cris.html (Date accessed 12 August 1997).

Stallard, C. 1974, 'An analysis of the writing behaviour of good student writers and their social setting', *Research in the Teaching of English*, vol. 3, no. 3, pp. 84–90.

Vici, V. 1996a, 'Vini italiani', *L'internazionale*, vol. 5, no. 1, pp. 2–20.

—— 1996b, 'French wines', *Harvest Magazine*, vol. 6, no. 4, pp. 13–22.

Wajcman, J. 1994, 'Technological A/genders: Technology, culture and class', in *Framing Technology: Society, Choice and Change*, L. Green & R. Guinery (eds), Allen & Unwin, Sydney.

Footnote/endnote system

As mentioned, the bibliography (see box on the next page) would be identical to the footnote or endnote citations listed in the referencing section of this chapter. The only difference is that the author's surname appears at the beginning, so that the references can be put in alphabetical order.

Annotated bibliography

An annotated bibliography contains full references, as in a bibliography, with the addition of brief descriptive notes providing evaluative comments on the work. It is important to write

FOOTNOTE/ENDNOTE SYSTEM

Australian Government Publishing Service, *Style Manual: For Authors, Editors and Printers*, 5th edn, AGPS, Canberra, 1994.

Nsure, S., *Learning Research*, Park Press, Melbourne, 1997.

Rong, P., *Introducing Learning*, Griffin Press, London, 1994.

—— *Memory and Learning*, Griffin Press, London, 1995.

Simple, R., 'Jumping tricks', *Croft Adventures*, V. 2 [CD-ROM], Micro-hard Corporation, 1994.

Vici, V., 'Vini italiani', *L'internazionale*, vol. 5, no. 1, 1996a, pp. 2–20.

—— 'French wines', *Harvest Magazine*, vol. 6, no. 4, 1996b, pp. 13–22.

Wright, J., *Learning and Empowerment*, Hard Knocks University Press, Preston, 1989.

this bibliography from the perspective of the relevance of each source listed to the topic of your assignment. This type of bibliography can be arranged either alphabetically or by topic.

Figure 8.5 is an example that can be used as a guide. Note that the citation follows the Harvard referencing style.

Figure 8.5 Sample annotated bibliography entry

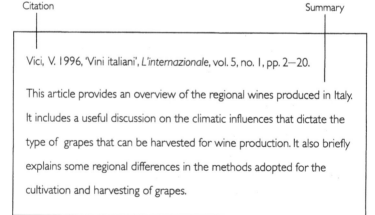

Citation   Summary

Vici, V. 1996, 'Vini italiani', *L'internazionale*, vol. 5, no. 1, pp. 2—20.

This article provides an overview of the regional wines produced in Italy. It includes a useful discussion on the climatic influences that dictate the type of grapes that can be harvested for wine production. It also briefly explains some regional differences in the methods adopted for the cultivation and harvesting of grapes.

CONCLUSION

Referencing conventions are formulaic and very strict. It is important to take care when referencing, making sure all the details are included with appropriate punctuation. Consistency is also vital. As technological resources are being adopted increasingly in scholastic work, conventions as to the use of these will evolve and become clearer.

✓ CHECKLIST FOR REFERENCING

☐ The referencing system you have used is the one recommended by your lecturer.

☐ All sources have been referenced.

☐ Exact wording, punctuation etc. have been respected in the direct quote.

☐ The quotes you have used support the argument rather than just embellish it.

☐ The quotes make sense when you read the whole text (if required, you have adjusted the quote using grammatical items or words to assist the reader in understanding the text).

☐ The sources of your quotes appear in the references list or bibliography.

☐ Only one style of referencing has been used, and there is no jumping between different styles.

☐ Sources have been copied correctly.

☐ If using the footnote system, the sources are numbered in the order they appear in the text.

☐ Each footnote (if used) is separated by a double line.

☐ Journal references include volume and issue number, if applicable.

☐ References for electronic sources detail the type of medium used.

☐ References for Web sites include the date accessed.

☐ Details appear in alphabetical order according to surnames.

☐ The edition is clearly identified.

☐ The text is cited according to the original language.

☐ Alphabetical notes distinguish two publications in one year by the same author (e.g. 1996a, 1996b).

9

Giving presentations

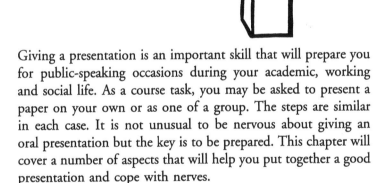

Giving a presentation is an important skill that will prepare you for public-speaking occasions during your academic, working and social life. As a course task, you may be asked to present a paper on your own or as one of a group. The steps are similar in each case. It is not unusual to be nervous about giving an oral presentation but the key is to be prepared. This chapter will cover a number of aspects that will help you put together a good presentation and cope with nerves.

AIMS OF A PRESENTATION

A presentation, just like a written task, gives you the opportunity to develop an argument. However, here you share the information in a way that is interesting and informative to a live audience rather than to a reader. It allows you to practise your public-speaking skills and lets the audience become involved by asking questions and making comments. The lecturer will review how well you prepare and deliver your topic. Some of the criteria that may be used in the assessment of the presentation are included in appendix 7.

STEPS IN PREPARING A GENERAL PRESENTATION

A presentation is structured in a similar way to a written text, with an introduction, body and conclusion.

The introduction

This should present, first, what you are going to talk about; second, some brief background detail about the relevance or importance of the issue; and third, the steps you will be taking during your presentation. The introduction is the moment when you capture the attention of the audience and present your topic. You should especially try to make a good first impression so that everyone, including your lecturer, sits up and takes notice. If there have been a number of presentations before you, this is particularly important. Some ways of doing this are to use a catchy phrase or quote, a question to the audience, an anecdote, a cartoon, or another relevant visual aid (remember, a picture is worth a 1000 words) (see box below). A good start will also help settle your nerves for the rest of the presentation.

STRATEGIES TO CATCH THE AUDIENCE'S ATTENTION

- a cartoon
- a picture
- a question for the audience
- a quote
- a short piece of film
- an anecdote
- a catchy phrase

The body

This part of a presentation contains the main argument of the talk. Important issues relating to the argument and an explanation as to their relevance should be included. You must include your evidence or results for each of the issues presented just as you would in a report or essay.

Using signalling phrases and connectives helps link ideas so that the whole argument flows smoothly from one idea to another. This also helps the audience keep track of the argument and remain interested. The box below gives some examples of linking phrases.

LINKING PHRASES	
Signal the start of an idea	• The argument centres around ... • The issues are based on ... • To begin with ...
Signal a move to the next idea	• We have outlined the arguments regarding ... so we can now turn our attention to ... • Having reviewed ... we can look at ... • We've seen how ... how about ...? • Understanding the argument just outlined will help us understand ...
Signal the end of one idea	• In brief, it has been demonstrated ... • All of this demonstrates ... • So we have seen ...
Indicate sequence	• First, second, third
Use connective phrases	• See appendix 6

The conclusion

The conclusion should be presented in a manner that makes an impact on the audience. It is important to summarise the key elements of the argument—that is, to take the audience back over the essential aspects stated. It is just as important to leave the audience with something to think about in regard to the topic as it is to start the whole presentation off well. Here again, you could use the same strategies as for the introduction— such as a cartoon, a quote or a question.

STEPS IN PREPARING A GENERAL PRESENTATION

Title
* title of the topic
* name of presenter(s)
* course name
* date presented

Introduction
* definition of the topic and the relevance of the topic to the course etc.
* statement of the main ideas you will be presenting
* outline of the steps of the presentation

Issue number 1
* presentation of the issue
* inclusion of supporting arguments or evidence

Issue number 2
* presentation of the issue
* inclusion of supporting arguments or evidence

Issues number 3
* presentation of the issue
* inclusion of supporting arguments or evidence

Conclusion
* summary of the key points of the argument
* strong statement about the argument

Question time

Question time

At the end of a presentation, students and the lecturer may ask you questions about aspects of the topic. This is a good chance to explain some points in more detail if necessary. When you answer these questions, make sure you retain eye contact. Look at the whole audience rather than just the person who asked the question, so that everyone feels involved. Sometimes questions are asked that require more detailed or broad information than your topic allows. It is acceptable in these circumstances to explain that further research would need to be accessed before you give an appropriate answer. Don't think you have to answer every possible question on the topic.

PREPARING A PRESENTATION: REPORT

Preparing a presentation which is a report on events or research involves certain different elements from a general presentation. While the aim of the introduction and conclusion are similar to that of a general presentation, the body covers different points. The first is the background to the topic: details of who was involved in carrying out the research for the report; the relevance of the topic and any other necessary background details. The second section is concerned with methodology: steps in undertaking the research are detailed, where the information was obtained, who the subjects were (if any), the timeline involved and so on. The third section outlines the findings on the topic: here, interesting aspects you want the audience to note need to be presented.

The next section is a brief outline of suggestions for any areas that require further research. Often, while you are undertaking research and are in the process of addressing one or two questions, other questions arise. This is an opportunity to demonstrate your critical thinking skills in analysing the topic in a broad context. Here, you may present thoughts, alternative steps or means to research such a topic. You can also include any problems that occurred in gathering your information and how you resolved them, if this was possible. This is not to say that the process was not correct, but that you have considered the whole process and come up with alternatives based on your experiences. The box below summarises the steps outlined that will assist you in preparing your presentation.

PREPARING FOR A PRESENTATION: REPORT

Title visual, including
- title of the topic
- name of presenter(s)
- course name
- date presented

Introduction
- definition of the topic
- list of the main points of the argument

Background to the topic
- explanation of who was involved
- description of why the topic was chosen, its relevance to the course/importance to society etc.

Methodology
- outline of steps you took in undertaking your research
- explanation of timeline or schedule of the project

Findings
- description of what you found out about the topic

Recommendations
- suggestions regarding areas that need further research or issues that have arisen from your work
- outline of problems you encountered and how you resolved them (if possible)

Conclusion
- summary of key points
- strong statement regarding your topic

Question time

SELECTING A TOPIC

Sometimes the topic is provided but if you have to choose one, select a topic in which you are really interested. It is much easier to research and present a lively talk about something that interests you rather than about something you do not understand or that you find boring.

PREPARING SLIDES AND OHTs

Giving an oral presentation does not mean reading straight from your notes. It is important that you arrange your written notes in a way that will help you deliver a structured argument that contains all the points you need to make *without* reading directly from your notes. Otherwise, eye contact is lost, the voice drops as you hold your head down to read, you do not sound so interesting, and the presentation is not so spontaneous.

Slides are a great way of both prompting your memory on aspects you want to cover and focusing the audience's attention on your main points. Programs such as Powerpoint allow you to create effective slides with pictures, graphs and video. If it is not possible to present the slides using a computer and projector, slides can be printed out and photocopied onto overhead transparencies (OHTs)—remember to make sure an overhead projector is provided for the class. Preparation of even a few attractive slides or OHTs will liven up your presentation and provide a positive stimulus for the audience.

PRACTISING YOUR PRESENTATION

It is important to practise reading over your notes with your slides, to gauge time allocation, voice control, body language, and help you memorise important points and slide sequence.

Practise the presentation by speaking aloud as you will do during the presentation session. This will help you ascertain the amount of time you can spend on each section. Writing the time down for each section on your notes helps you keep track of time during the presentation. Speaking aloud will also assist you to develop the right sort of tone for the talk and gets you used to the sound of your own voice, particularly if English is not your first language. Remember, in an English-speaking culture an important point is highlighted by a pause, a slower pace and a slightly raised voice.

Body language is both personal and cultural. English-speakers use body language to help in the communication process: for instance, it is used to emphasise certain words. Leaning forward slightly over the table and looking at the audience helps create an air of intimacy, of something that is being shared with the listener. Eye contact is essential, as discussed in previous chapters: it sends out a message of honesty, knowledge and confidence. It also helps maintain the interest of the audience. If you do not look at the audience members, they probably will not look at you!

Coping with nerves

Being nervous is a natural reaction to standing up in front of peers. If you are prepared and are confident in what and how you are going to present, the process will be much easier. Your nervousness will stimulate you to try your best. If you are really nervous, try deep-breathing exercises beforehand. Smile to yourself (and the audience) before you start. During the time you move from one slide to another, take two or three deep breaths and keep positive. Have a drink of water on the table nearby in case your throat feels dry. Taking a sip also gives you time to take a deep breath and keep a positive focus. If eye contact is difficult because it makes you feel even more nervous, try looking just above everyone's heads. Having an encouraging friend sitting in the audience can help also.

GROUP PRESENTATIONS

The information in this chapter on preparing and delivering a presentation will help you plan and prepare a group presentation also. The steps in preparing the presentation are a little different from planning one individually. The key is to plan the presentation as a group, making sure everyone has an equal amount of work—also, to ensure that there are opportunities to practise as a group. The box below is a planning guide.

POSSIBLE STEPS IN PRESENTING AS A GROUP

First meeting

1. Meet together to discuss the topic and list points (brainstorm).
2. Group the points under key issues/headings.
3. Work out how much time, roughly, should be allocated to each issue.
4. Allocate research and writing-up tasks among the members of the group.
5. Work out your handouts.
6. Plan your slides.

Second meeting

1. Go over the main issues that will be presented, making sure it is all included.
2. Go over your supporting arguments and evidence.
3. Make sure the introduction and conclusion are clear and effective.
4. Make sure there are links between each other's sections, e.g.
   • As my colleague has stated . . .
   • As has been mentioned . . .
5. Check the overheads and handouts.
6. Think about possible questions you may be asked—and answers.
7. Practise the presentation as a group. You will probably need to practise this a few times.

CONCLUSION

Students naturally get nervous about presentations. It feels as if you are being put on a stage for both peers and staff to analyse. However, it is important to stay focused and relaxed. Ensure that you have three clear sections—the introduction, the body, and the conclusion. If possible, prepare some visual stimulus to keep the audience's attention focused. If you have prepared your presentation there should be no reason not to do well: just remain confident. After all, everyone wants you to do well, as they want to hear and see an interesting and informative presentation.

✓ CHECKLIST FOR ORAL PRESENTATIONS

☐ Is the introduction clear, concise and strong?

☐ Are sections presented in a logical order?

☐ Do the main points stand out?

☐ Does each main point have supporting ideas?

☐ Does the conclusion sum up ideas?

☐ Does the presentation have a strong conclusion?

☐ Does the talk flow nicely?

☐ Are the overheads clear and relevant?

☐ Are there too many overheads?

☐ Are the handouts complete and presented well?

☐ Is the timing of the presentation accurate?

☐ Are all the notes and overheads in order?

☐ Have you rehearsed the presentation?

☐ Do you feel confident?

10

Organising study time

Managing your time during your studies is an important part of the whole learning process. Planning your time effectively means that you need to consider all your activities—not just your study situation. A timetable assists in time management but it needs to reflect real time, not ideal time. Make sure it is a good working document for *you*. Your timetable will be dictated by your classes and assignments. Here, two schedules are suggested. One is your weekly timetable and the other is a semester schedule. You may need to organise your work, social and family commitments as well as your studies. Just as in a work situation, study time should be organised in order to ensure that deadlines are met, stress is reduced and that the learning process can occur in an effective and efficient way. At first, you may seem to have a lot of spare time after you block out times for classes, but you need to remember that you will be required to prepare for classes and assignments.

WEEKLY STUDY SCHEDULE

You will probably find that a weekly study schedule is easy to organise initially as class times are given to you by your lecturers, however, you need to allocate times to work on class tasks and research, essay preparation and other tasks.

When planning your weekly schedule, it is important to be realistic about the amount of time *you* need to study. Everyone works at a different pace. Also, you will need breaks and spare time to pursue your favourite activities. You will need time to see your friends and visit places. If you study all the time you will get tired and will be unable to concentrate effectively. Having a break and doing something you enjoy means less stress and a fresh beginning every time you pick up your books. Figure 10.1 is an example of a weekly timetable for you to use as a guide. Note how the study time is spread out over the day and evening, so that you can pursue activities and not work late into the night when your energy levels are low. (Appendix 8 is a blank copy of a weekly schedule for you to copy and use for your studies.)

SEMESTER STUDY SCHEDULE

Your semester study schedule will require a lot more forward planning. You need to review all your assessment requirements, exams, any religious or family events and allocate research time every week accordingly. Figure 10.2 is an example. The ability to plan and organise your time will help in taking the stress out of study. (Appendix 9 is a blank copy of a semester schedule for you to copy and use.)

Planning problems

If your planning and schedule are not working out, do not get worried. On some days, matters will arise that distract you from your studies. If you have to reschedule your study time in the

Figure 10.1 Weekly study schedule

Time	Monday	Tuesday	Wednesday	Thursday	Friday	Saturday	Sunday
9.00–10.00	Lecture: Accounting	Library research	Computer room. Prepare tasks for computer applications	Tutorial: Management and organisational behaviour	Tutorial: Accounting	Free time	Reading
10.00–10.30	Break		Break	Break	Tutorial: Tourism	Shopping	
10.30–11.00	Review notes for tutorial	Break	Research	Tutorial: Computer applications	Break		
11.00–12.30	Tutorial: Financial management	Lecture: Tourism			Research	Gym etc.	
12.30–1.30	Lunch	Lunch	Lunch	Lunch	Lunch	Lunch	Lunch
1.30–3.00	Library. Tutorial preparation	Lecture: Financial management	Tutorial: Tourism	Research	Tutorial: Applied economics	Revision	Social activities
3.00–4.00	Lecture: Management and organisational behaviour	Tutorial: Computer applications	Research	Lectures: Applied economics	Research	Revision	
4.00–5.00	Study group: Management and organisational behaviour	Tutorial: Accounting	Tutorial: Accounting	Applied economics study group meeting	Gym	Evening social activities	
5.00–7.00	Dinner & relaxation	Dinner & relaxation	Dinner & relaxation	Dinner & relaxation	Dinner & relaxation		
7.00–9.30	Review class notes. Reading and note-taking	Review class notes. Tutorial tasks	Gym	Review class notes. Reading.	Free evening		Preparation for week

Figure 10.2 Semester study schedule

Semester (weeks)	Accounting	Financial management	Management and organisational behaviour
1	Planning and literature search. Take notes	Planning and literature search for essay	Meet students in study group to brainstorm ideas for case study
2	Complete section A. Tutorial assignment	Note-taking for essay	Reading for case study. Note-taking. Draft case study.
3	Complete sections B & C. Tutorial assignment	Complete first draft for essay	Redraft case study and submit. **Case study due**
4	Redraft and submit. **Tutorial assignment due**	Complete second draft and check references	General reading
5	Literature search. Notes. Tutorial assignment	Edit and submit. **Essay due**	Planning of oral presentation with group. Literature search
6	Complete sections A & B. Tutorial assignment	Revise topics 1–3	Initial reading and note-taking. Second meeting with group to organise points.
7	Complete section C. Redraft. Tutorial assignment	Revise topics 4–6	Revise presentation. Practice.
8	Submit. **Tutorial assignment due**	Practice exams	Oral presentation/practice. **Oral presentation due**
9	Literature search. Tutorial assignment	Revise topics 7–9	Planning of case study. Literature search
10	Complete sections A & B. Tutorial assignment	Practice exams	Reading and note-taking
11	Complete section C. Redraft assignment	Revise topics 10–11	First draft of case study
12	**Tutorial assignment due**	Practice exams and revision	Second draft of case study
13	**End of semester**	**Exams**	Edit and submit. **Case Study due**

evening because of an important football match, then do so. Enjoy yourself and make up the time later. As long as the schedule is working generally, you should be fine. If, on the whole, the schedule does not seem to be working, revise it to reflect your own study style. For instance, if you are more comfortable with beginning your studies early in the morning, arrange your planning to reflect this. Also, you need to avoid the tendency to put things off to another time, that is, *procrastinate*. It is easy to do when things are difficult, or boring, or you are tired.

MOTIVATION

At some point during your studies you may not really feel motivated and your interest in attending classes or working on your tasks may be low. Sometimes a day spent on a favourite activity will help 'recharge the batteries', while at other times it takes a little more. One way of attacking the feeling of stagnation is breaking up what you have to do when planning your everyday tasks. Review the tasks and write them down as a list, for example in your diary:

THINGS TO DO   **15 MARCH 1999**

☐ Read chapter 5.
☐ Revise notes.
☐ Do numbers 1–3 of accounting tutorial task.

Once you have finished each task put a tick next to it, enjoy the feeling of accomplishment, and reward yourself—perhaps by taking a walk or watching a TV show afterwards.

When motivation is low it is also easy to skip classes, however not attending classes will only worsen the problem. Stay focused and try to remain positive about your everyday accomplishments. If the lack of motivation becomes a real problem you

Time management tips

- *Use the day wisely: do not leave all your work for the evening. Spread it out.*
- *Make sure you include breaks so you are under less stress and can return to your tasks with a fresh approach.*
- *Vary your study tasks during the day: working on just one subject can make you feel tired and bored.*
- *Work at home and the library: a change of study environment can help break the routine.*
- *Write up and use a realistic study schedule.*
- *Ensure that your friends and family know your social times so you are less likely to be disturbed during study times.*

may need to speak to a counsellor before, as a result of anxiety or stress, you lose too much valuable time in your studies or your health suffers. A counsellor will work out some beneficial strategies that are designed just for you.

CONCLUSION

Developing good time management skills will prove an asset during your studies. Using schedules helps focus your study time so that a lot of time between classes and evenings is not wasted. Schedules should be realistic and leave spare time to relax—otherwise they become too restrictive and tend to affect your motivation levels negatively. In the end, you can spend many hours at your desk but if your motivation is low and you are tired, this may be a useless exercise. Balancing your activities and keeping a positive attitude will help you maintain good time management skills.

Using the library

It is important that you get to know your library well. This means understanding how the library catalogue works, where books, journals, audiovisual equipment and other resources are located, how to use the computer CD-ROM research facilities, how to book equipment, study rooms, and so on. All academic libraries conduct tours for students and staff; also, there are librarians on duty at the information desk to assist with queries.

LIBRARY STRUCTURE

Library tours

Library tours are aimed at familiarising students with the layout of the library—where different sections are located, the types of different resources available and how to access resources. After the tour, take time to familiarise yourself with the library catalogue system and the area in which the materials for your discipline are kept.

Catalogue systems

The most commonly used item in the library is the library catalogue, which lists all the library resources and where each is located. Most catalogues are now computer-based. A common mistake made by students is going to the library catalogue system unsure about what they need to locate. Searching can then be a long, tedious task. Before you start your search, think about your topic, important key words, any particular dates or locations that limit your search and so on. The catalogue system allows you to do searches by:

- title of book
- author's name
- author/title
- subject
- key word (in title)
- call number.

These computer systems are easy to use. Once you have been shown how, you will pick it up with a little practice and by following the on-screen instructions. The computer lists a number of materials quite efficiently—that is, journals, audio, visual and text-based materials. Each item contains information as to its location in the library by a *call number*. You need to note down this number to locate the item on the shelves. The screen also gives you information on whether the text has been borrowed and when it is due back. If it has been borrowed you may 'place a hold' on it, so that, when it is returned, the librarian will put it aside for you. Figure 11.1 is an example of a subject search for 'essay'.

The catalogue prompts you to insert information so that the search can begin. In Figure 11.2 the word 'essay' is typed in under the heading *Subject*. The catalogue looks for resources that deal with this subject.

In Figure 11.3, the student chooses to look at the first text,

Figure 11.1   Sample subject search

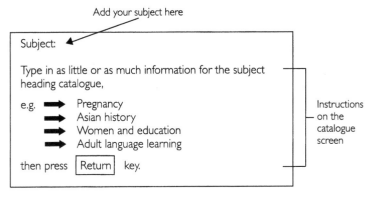

Add your subject here

Subject:

Type in as little or as much information for the subject heading catalogue,

e.g.   ➡   Pregnancy
       ➡   Asian history
       ➡   Women and education
       ➡   Adult language learning

then press   Return   key.

Instructions on the catalogue screen

Figure 11.2   Choices from the catalogue

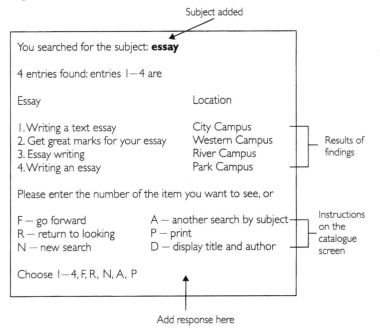

Subject added

You searched for the subject: **essay**

4 entries found: entries 1—4 are

Essay   Location

1. Writing a text essay   City Campus
2. Get great marks for your essay   Western Campus
3. Essay writing   River Campus
4. Writing an essay   Park Campus

Results of findings

Please enter the number of the item you want to see, or

F — go forward   A — another search by subject
R — return to looking   P — print
N — new search   D — display title and author

Instructions on the catalogue screen

Choose 1—4, F, R, N, A, P

Add response here

'Writing a text essay', so number 1 is selected. The catalogue then searches for information on this particular item and comes up with details showing that this item is a video recording which lasts for 22 minutes. There is a summary of the content, which indicates where the item can be located on the shelves by matching the call number. The catalogue indicates that it is available for borrowing for a period of up to seven days.

Figure 11.3   Information on choice from catalogue

You searched for the subject: **essay**

Title   Writing a text essay [video recording]

Author   Video Classroom

Publisher   Richmond [VIC]:Video Classroom, 1992

Physical description   1 video cassette (22 minutes)

Subject   Essay — techniques
              English language

Summary   Shows how to write an essay about a text without retelling
              the story. Explains planning, writing parts of an essay.

Series   English (video classroom)

Location	Call Number	Status
City 7 day	808.042 WRI	Available

R — return to looking   A — another search by subject
B — backward   S — show similar items
N — new search   Q — request item

Choose one (1, R, B, N, A, S, Q)

Add your instructions

Library counters/desks

There are various desks located in the library. The *main desk* is usually where you borrow books or equipment. The *information desk* is staffed by people who will answer your queries about using the library and help you to find materials. At the *reserve desk* you will find materials that subject lecturers have put on restricted access. This happens when there is a high demand for certain items and borrowing time must be limited to a few hours or overnight. The staff are available to assist you in your queries so do not feel uncomfortable about approaching them and asking questions.

Online literature search

These searches of databases occur online. This means you can be sitting in a library in Melbourne and access a database in a Parisian library. The online literature searches are usually discipline-based, so there are searches specifically for engineering, marketing, literature and so on. The library at your institution will have a guide regarding online literature searches available in your discipline.

LIBRARY SECTIONS

Reference section

General texts such as encyclopaedias, dictionaries, maps, indexes and atlases are found in the reference section. These are not available for loan, as normally they are needed only briefly by the user.

Journals section

Specialist 'magazines' for different disciplines are called *journals* or *periodicals*. These contain up-to-date discussions and research into specialist areas and so are a good way to keep up with current information. Journals are kept in a separate section of the library and normally can be used only in the library rather than borrowed. If you are unsure about the journals available in your area of study, ask for suggestions from your lecturer or librarian. As a postgraduate research student, you may be able to access articles from journals that are not located at your institution through the *interlibrary loan* process (by which material requested at one library is sent by another library in Australia or overseas).

Databases

Technology now allows huge records and lists of information to be stored on CD-ROM (CD Read Only Memory) databases. These are very helpful, particularly at a postgraduate research level. The librarian will show you how to access and interpret the information you need. Normally, you will be able to get printouts of useful information. There are different CD-ROMs for different disciplines. The box below contains a list of some useful databases.

RESEARCH DATABASES

APAIS—Australian Public Affairs Information Service

Austrom—Collection of Australian databases on various subjects, such as education, language teaching, social sciences and architecture

ERIC—Education

Australian Tourism Index—Tourism and hospitality

CINAHL—Medicine and health sciences

Medline—Medical

Psyclit—Psychology

Sociofile—Sociology

Sport Discus—Sport/physical education

Audiovisual section

Tapes, CDs and videos are available from the audiovisual section. These can be used in a specific area of the library or borrowed.

Newspaper section

Newspapers from different states and countries are available in university libraries. These allow you to keep up with news and to review information that may be useful to your field.

Microfiche and microfilm section

Microfiche and microfilm contain materials that have been reduced photographically—for instance, old newspapers, government documents and old journals. The film can be read on special readers that magnify the text; these are also available in the library.

Computer section

Computers are set aside for student use. These usually have to be booked in advance. Computers will have different software packages, so you should check with the librarian if you need something in particular. Usually they can be used to access the Internet and word-process documents. (The computer laboratories also give you access to computer equipment.)

Photocopying section

Photocopiers are kept in one section which you can use with a card. Some libraries have photocopy cards which you can buy which allow you to copy a particular number of pages: for instance, a $10 card may allow you to photocopy 65 copies. Others allow you to use your student card, which you load with a certain amount of money. The librarian will show you how to do this.

ACCESSING THE LIBRARY VIA THE NET

Some libraries can now be accessed via the Internet. You will be able to get information and a demonstration of how this works at your institution by asking the librarian. It means that you can use the facilities of your library—such as searching for resources, holding an item and renewing a book—without going into the library in person. Also, ask about how to search other university libraries using this facility. It makes study faster than visiting different libraries physically to find a particular item.

USING RESOURCES FROM OTHER LIBRARIES

Academic libraries

You will be able to access materials at other academic libraries. You may even borrow materials by organising a special card at your own institution's library and then presenting it at other libraries.

If you are doing postgraduate studies, it may be possible to order books from other tertiary institutions through an *inter-library loan* process. You will need to complete a form detailing the material needed and submit it to the appropriate librarian, who will access it for you to borrow just as any other library book. Be aware that you need to plan ahead, as such a process can take a number of weeks.

Public and state libraries

Public libraries are located in the suburbs, while state libraries are usually in or near the city centre. You can use these libraries without any charge. Specialist libraries, such as the Institution of Engineers library, may require you to be a member or present a letter from your department stating that you are enrolled in an engineering course. Each specialist library has its own regulations. Check with staff, explaining your situation, and they may be able to help.

CONCLUSION

The library is an important storehouse of information and resources. Studying can be made easier and more time-efficient by gaining a familiarity with the types of resources located there. It takes time to build up a knowledge of these, but the staff are there to assist you if you have any problems using or locating resources.

12

Assessment

Assessment at tertiary level is not usually based on exams alone. It is often based on work submitted throughout the year, exams and class participation. Some courses do not include exams, and base assessment mainly on assignments. Postgraduate research students, particularly at master's level, are assessed in part or completely on the research project submitted.

WHAT IS ASSESSMENT?

Assignments may include reports, essays, practicals, oral presentations, research projects, designs, pieces of artwork or a mixture of these. At the start of the course, each of your subject lecturers will tell you what is expected and how many points are allocated to each task. You may also get hints on how to set out your task, or the lecturer may drop a few hints during the course. Either way, ask the lecturer to explain if something is not clear.

Assessment has an important role in tertiary studies. It gives both lecturer and student a record of course objectives that have been fulfilled and areas of improvement. At the completion of each stage in the course there is a record of your readiness to progress to a higher level.

In addition, assessment records are used in a professional context—for instance, when applying for a job or joining a professional body. Some graffiti on a university wall stated: 'I don't care what marks I get, I just want to finish this course and get out of here!'. The feeling of depression is not uncommon during a long course. However, it is important to *care:* apathy will not help you achieve your best and low results could hinder you in getting the position you want. Caring about doing the *best you can* to help you fulfil your assessment tasks and study objectives is more profitable than apathy.

Usually you will have some idea about your own progress. Rather than waiting for feedback from your lecturers, it is important to gauge your own progress in a realistic manner. Sometimes self-assessment will help you keep on track. Assess your own areas of strengths and weaknesses. The box below gives a self-assessment checklist to help you think about progress and ways to improve.

SELF-ASSESSMENT CHECKLIST

- [ ] What were my goals at the beginning of my studies?
- [ ] If these have changed, how have they changed?
- [ ] What are my strengths in my studies (e.g. critical thinking, writing)?
- [ ] What are my weaknesses in my studies?
- [ ] What have I done to tackle my weaknesses (e.g. read every day, take up conversation classes, do an essay-writing course)?
- [ ] What do I still have to do to tackle my weaknesses?
- [ ] With whom do I feel comfortable talking about study skills improvement?

EXAM PREPARATION

Depending on the course you do, you may find that you are required to do exams. In the Australian tertiary system it is not always necessary. Also, a pass or fail for the course does not usually depend only on your performance in exams: other evidence of participation and programs is normally taken into account.

While there are different types of exams, the key to successful exams is *preparation*. This does not mean *cramming* a week before exams but attending lectures, good note-taking, critical thinking throughout the semester or year, constantly revising and becoming familiar with the subjects in order to be confident with the arguments. Give yourself plenty of time to prepare for exams.

How to prepare for exams

The box on the next page gives a quick check to help you think about your own style of exam preparation. Doing this check and reading the advice below may help you improve on your exam preparation techniques.

Swotvac

'Swotvac' is the period between the time classes finish and exams begin. This time is set aside for students to prepare for exams. A timetable will be available a few weeks before swotvac so that you can prepare an exam study schedule around exam dates.

Exam study schedule

Planning a schedule is like planning your study timetable (see chapter 10). Study periods and relaxation times both need to be included. Also, balance the time you spend on each subject. You may have a subject in which you are not so strong, so you may allocate more time to that subject; however, do not neglect other subjects.

Study periods include making revision notes, reading and doing practice exams. Each task needs to be planned and systematic. Vary the tasks each day so that you do not get bored. Leave time at the end of each task to recall important material. Recalling may mean writing out a summary, a list of points, a chart, speaking aloud, or meeting friends to discuss and check issues.

Reviewing your notes

During your exam preparation time, review your class notes, notes from readings and written tasks. Make summaries of your notes on each topic as you go as this will help with memorising important points and thinking about issues. Reading your notes aloud can also help with memorisation. In your study group, you can use these notes to guide your discussions, particularly if you are going through past exams.

DIFFERENT TYPES OF EXAMS

There are different types of exams and different tasks that may be required. This can be disconcerting if you are used to taking a particular type of exam and are given something different. In some cultures oral exams are common: in Europe, for instance, these may be quite lengthy and detailed and a majority of marks for the course may be allocated to these exams alone. In Asia, multiple-choice exams are common. For both European and Asian systems generally, memorisation plays an integral role in preparing for exams.

In Australia, exams may be multiple-choice, essay-based, include short-answer questions, or contain a mixture of question types. Exams vary in style too: there are the standard exams, where you rely mainly on memory and critical thinking skills, and *open-book exams*, where you are permitted to bring in textbooks and sometimes notes. Here you do not have to memorise details but can concentrate on the argument. For example, in a literature exam, textbook and notes can be referred to for important short quotes; in law exams, texts can help when you need to refer to a statute. You may get a *take-home exam* to complete overnight, or over a couple of days. Contrary to some student beliefs, these exams are not easy: they require as much preparation and concentrated work as any other major assignment.

Multiple-choice exams

Multiple-choice exams consist of lots of statements or questions each with a list of four or five possible answers from which you need to choose the most appropriate one. The wording of each multiple-choice question needs to be carefully noted. Often there are two seemingly right answers and only a slight difference in meaning separates the two. Significant words might be 'always', 'often', 'never', 'very'. Read all the alternatives carefully before making a selection. If you are not sure, circle the one you think is correct and put an asterisk next to it. It is better to have a try—just in case you do not get around to reviewing your answers at the end of the exam—than to leave blank questions. If you are short of time at the end, at least you have indicated the important questions to check and can concentrate on these.

Short-answer questions

The answers to these questions vary in length. In some exams you are expected to write a few words as an answer, while in others a few paragraphs are required. If you do need to write a statement of a few paragraphs, just as in an essay-based exam, a plan can help keep you focused on the question. Bear in mind the rules for writing: have a clear introduction, discussion and conclusion. If the main body of the answer is only a paragraph or two in length, a sentence may suffice as introduction and conclusion.

PRACTICE EXAMS

Practice exams can be used to train yourself to work under the pressure of exam conditions and revise material. A few weeks before your exam, go through past exam papers. Your lecturer, department office or library will have these. Review the papers to see what type of questions are asked, how many questions of each type are included, how points are allocated to each, the number of sections and what types of instruction words are used. Doing past exams can give you useful information and practice. Your lecturers will be able to tell you whether the format of present exams is similar.

Analysing the question

Begin analysing the question by focusing on key words and instruction words (see appendix 4). Read what the question is asking, not what *you think* it is asking. Jot down your notes on a 'scratch paper'—that is, a sheet of paper for your rough notes or brainstorming ideas.

Time allocation

Just as you would under normal exam conditions, set an amount of time to answering each question and stick to the time allocated. At first you may find it difficult to complete the task in the time set, but as you practise this will become easier.

Self-assessment

At the end of each practice exam session or after a day or two (if time permits), assess your work just as an examiner would. Your notes will help you with this process. Look at your work critically. Ask yourself whether the question has been answered. Tick the points that are valid and check to see whether any have been omitted. Using a different-coloured pen, correct your work and add any important points. Another strategy is comparing and discussing reasons for answers with those in your study group, and whether these answers have been expressed clearly.

Planning your answer

Having a plan for your answer helps you focus on a question and give a relevant and logical answer. Write out your plan as you would normally, with an introduction, body and conclusion. In an exam situation, a brief but neatly written plan will demonstrate what you know to a lecturer in case you do not finish the exam. Lecturers sometimes look at your plans for an indication of what you would have written, and a few extra marks are better than none.

Reviewing

Leave time at the end to review your answers. Proofread the answers as you normally would, eliminating spelling, punctuation or expression errors.

Exam essays

In some exams you may be required to write essays. These will not be as polished as your other course essays, but that is to be expected. Instead, your recollection of main points—and ability to present your understanding through an argument, based around the instruction words—is examined.

Exam essays are written under pressure and particular preparation is needed, so past exams can be helpful. Using the same basic techniques as you would when writing an essay, try doing past exam essays under the pressure of time, scaling down to the period usually allocated in an exam so that you get used to working to a time limit. Writing out a brief plan for your essays will ensure that you stay focused on the exam question and do not diverge from it under the pressure of time. Also, leave 5–10 minutes at the end for editing.

DURING THE EXAM

Time during the exam needs to be allocated carefully to the various tasks, and you need to stay focused. This is easy to say but not always easy to do. The box on the next page will give you hints about what to do during exams.

The first 10–15 minutes in an exam is called *reading time*. In some exams you are allowed to jot down points, while others are strict about reading only. During this time, read all the questions carefully. *Read the question*, not what you *think* is the question. Remember to take note of instruction words and

THINKING ABOUT HOW YOU ACT DURING EXAMS, CIRCLE THE APPROPRIATE ANSWER.

• Do you allocate time to each different section and pace yourself?	Yes	No
• Do you get nervous and tense up so that you cannot think?	Yes	No
• Do you plan your answers (e.g. exam essays)?	Yes	No
• Do you take careful note of instruction words?	Yes	No
• Do you read over your exam answers with a 'critical eye'?	Yes	No
• Do you run out of time so that you end up scribbling towards the end of the paper?	Yes	No
• Do you leave out questions you are not sure about?	Yes	No
• Do you leave early?	Yes	No
• Do you look over your exam to make sure you have completed all the questions?	Yes	No

key words. If you are permitted to take notes, use this time to underline words. If relevant, write up quick plans which include allotting time to each question or section. Use the time wisely.

Select the questions you feel able to tackle and how much time to allocate to each. Do not make the common mistake of spending too much time on one question and then not having enough time for others. Stick to your time allocation and keep an eye on your watch. At the end of the essay or short-answer question, if you have not finished, you can jot down a few main points and go on to the next task. Use the review time left at the end of the exam to fill in more details if you can. If you do not get a chance to get back to it, your examiner may look at the points to gauge what you were trying to say and take this into consideration.

At the end of an exam, there is hardly ever enough time left for revising your work, but do not forget to proofread your answers, looking for simple errors in spelling and punctuation.

> ***Study tip*** *Have a 'planning sheet' on which you can quickly note down any ideas, key words, or do the planning for your exams, essays or short-answer questions.*

EXAM STRATEGIES

You will have your own style and methods for preparing for exams. Having exam strategies will help you perform well and cope with nerves. Exam strategies include:

- allocating time to tasks;
- getting materials organised and ready;
- preparing for case study or essay-based exams;
- allocating a review time towards the end of the exams;
- starting with the question you feel more at ease with, to help build up your confidence;
- writing neatly;
- attempting all questions;
- not wasting time fretting over difficult questions: do what you can and go on (you can come back to them at the end).

Coping with nerves

Nerves are a natural part of the excitement and tension before an important event. However, adrenalin can help you perform

BEFORE THE EXAMS

- Make sure you know where the exam is going to be held and the exact time.
- A bit of 'R&R' (rest and relaxation) the night before can often help *unstress* you. A good night's rest will help ensure that you are mentally alert for the next day.
- Organise your equipment—pencils, pens, calculators etc.

DURING THE EXAMS

- Do not leave any question unanswered. Write in what you can, even in point form: a few marks are better than none.
- Plan answers.
- Allow time at the end of the exam to proofread answers and eliminate simple errors.
- Do not spend the majority of the time doing only one or two questions: allocate your time wisely.

well under pressure. The key is to stay focused and remember your exam strategies. Do not panic! Knowing your work and having practised it is good preparation, so be confident. Closing your eyes and taking a few deep breaths whenever you feel you are getting anxious will help you focus again and get down to business.

> *Study tip*   *Revision is often done during the last classes of the semester or term, which is why it is important to attend classes rather than stay at home to revise. You may otherwise miss out on those all important last-minute hints from your lecturers.*

AFTER THE EXAMS

It is natural to feel worried, deflated and highly relieved once the exam is over. Once the time is up, leave the exam room and do something you enjoy as a treat. You have sat the exam, which is an accomplishment. Do not spend time alone or with friends worrying about your answers. Stay positive and enjoy the relief.

CONCLUSION

Assessment, particularly exams, causes a lot of anxiety. It is important to be prepared by maintaining a good study schedule throughout the course, which permits frequent revision rather than leaving all the studying to a week before the exams. Self-assessment will assist you in preparing for assessment tasks. By analysing your weak points you will give yourself more time to remedy these before the final submission or exam date.

Postgraduate studies

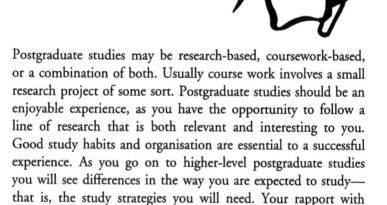

Postgraduate studies may be research-based, coursework-based, or a combination of both. Usually course work involves a small research project of some sort. Postgraduate studies should be an enjoyable experience, as you have the opportunity to follow a line of research that is both relevant and interesting to you. Good study habits and organisation are essential to a successful experience. As you go on to higher-level postgraduate studies you will see differences in the way you are expected to study—that is, the study strategies you will need. Your rapport with lecturers and supervisors will probably change also.

Attending classes

Seminars, tutorials and workshops may be part of postgraduate study, depending on the course. It is important to attend these classes and take part by asking questions and raising points for discussion. If another student or lecturer disagrees with your opinion, it is important to listen carefully and respond by developing your argument further. This can be done by providing further evidence, asking a question, or reiterating an important point. Discussion is seen to be 'healthy' and a part of participation in academic discourse.

Converting to a master's or doctorate

Many tertiary institutions offer postgraduate diplomas or certificates. These usually involve one year's full-time study. Sometimes the work you do in this course can be converted or credited to a master's-level course. Your progress is usually taken into account if this is requested. You should speak to the course supervisor about any intention to convert to a master's-level course. Similarly, a master's-level course may be converted to a doctorate-level course.

WHAT IS RESEARCH?

Research involves questioning and analysing the literature in a particular field, and adding further knowledge and discussion through information, experiences and ideas.

Types of research degrees vary: usually an honours, master's or PhD can be undertaken by research alone, or by a combination of research and coursework. Some higher education institutions offer a master's degree by coursework alone, but a research project often forms part of the requirements. A *thesis* or *dissertation* is a research study undertaken at a postgraduate level.

Why undertake research?

Research is undertaken for a variety of professional and personal reasons. Some students take up research studies because it is expected by their employer or to gain promotional opportunities in the workplace. Some undertake these studies as a result of parental pressure. Others may be interested in a particular field of study and want to be able to contribute to that field through research.

When you undertake research you will assess what is known about a particular field of study. You will identify key issues or a problem that requires investigation. A commonly referred-to objective of research studies is to make a *significant* contribution to a particular field. This does not necessarily mean an earth-shattering, intellectual study but a contribution to a field of study that is original and new in perspective, methodology or approach.

STEPS INVOLVED IN RESEARCH STUDIES

There are 12 steps (see box below) to organising your research studies. Each should be taken into account at the planning stage, and none should be omitted.

ORGANISING RESEARCH STUDIES

1. Read about an area in which you are interested to help you identify a question/topic.
2. Talk to lecturers or colleagues about the topic.
3. Identify a general question.
4. Choose and consult a supervisor for your research.
5. Write up a brief research proposal to submit with your candidature application.
6. Plan your research project.
7. Undertake a literature search.
8. Identify an appropriate research method.
9. Collect data.
10. Interpret the data.
11. Do final write up of research study.
12. Submit your research project.

How to identify a research question

It is important to keep up to date with the literature in your chosen field of study. From your reading you will be able to assess areas that need further investigation. Your supervisor will also assist you with reading material and suggestions.

You need to decide on the feasibility and relevance of the topic. Choose a topic that is manageable: do not try to write an encyclopaedia on the topic. You need to be very careful about choosing a focused question that you can manage. Your interest in the topic is also essential. Research is hard work and if you choose a topic that is not motivating it will be even harder.

Your supervisor and you

The relationship between your supervisor and you is a vital ingredient of successful research studies. Just as any relationship, it may have its high and low points, so communication is important—especially if you are going to be studying over a period of years.

In Australia, it is customary to choose your own supervisor. Alternatively, you can be allocated one. If you decide to choose a supervisor, you need to think very carefully about your choice, on the basis of:

- the supervisor's knowledge of the area of study;
- the supervisor's experience;
- accessibility of the supervisor: it is useless having the most reputable person in the field if you never get a chance to see him/her;
- potential to strike up a comfortable rapport with the supervisor.

You may find that you have a supervisor and a co-supervisor, perhaps because the supervisor has a number of research commitments. Also, if your area of research crosses into other fields, two supervisors with strengths in different fields may be allocated to you.

Your supervisor will indicate areas of study, recommend reading, suggest other people that will assist you, ask questions that will help you explore your research topic, advise you in planning your work, ask you to define the aims of your research, and check that everything is progressing well and that your work is of an academic standard. To help your supervisor, ensure that the work you give him/her is legible, organised and on time.

A way to utilise meeting time is to prepare a list of questions on which to focus the discussion each meeting. Also, negotiate regular meeting times with your supervisor, ideally every fortnight. Give him/her a copy of the points and questions to be covered. As a student, it is important to be guided in the research by your supervisor.

Over a period of time it is usual for your relationship with your supervisor to change. At first he/she will instruct you on many aspects of the research study, sources of literature, research design and planning issues. As you undertake your reading, collecting and analysing of data, your supervisor will be there to facilitate this work and ensure that you are asking and answering the right questions. As you begin to write up your study you will become the specialist in the content; however, your supervisor will take an active role in commenting critically on your work.

Sometimes the relationship between a supervisor and a student breaks down, perhaps because the commitment of one or the other is not strong. It is important to discuss any difficulties together. If there is no improvement after a period of time, further action needs to be taken. The postgraduate research officer may offer helpful support and good advice on remedying the situation.

There are steps you can follow to ensure that both you and your supervisor have a positive research experience. The box on the next page lists some strategies for good supervision.

> **SOME STRATEGIES FOR GOOD SUPERVISION**
>
> - Set agreed-on meeting times with your supervisor during early discussions; appointments can vary between every week and every three weeks.
> - Keep to agreed meeting times and arrive on time.
> - Have something ready for the supervisor to read or discuss with him/her. You may need to initiate the direction of the meeting.
> - If you have promised to submit a draft of a chapter by a certain date, keep that date. If there is good reason not to, explain this to the supervisor: a phone call or e-mail will suffice.
> - Remember, supervisors need holidays too. Try to submit your drafts throughout the teaching semester, unless your supervisor is happy to read your work on the beach.

Writing up a brief research proposal

Each university has its own views on what is required for the research proposal that is attached to your *candidature application.* Consult the postgraduate officer in charge of your field of study to get details of the requirements for candidature and research proposals. (At some institutions there is one central office.) Your supervisor or the coordinator of the research studies program of your department is also there to help. Usually, you will need to provide a paragraph on each of the following:

- proposed title;
- focus of the study;
- the study's contribution to knowledge in the field;
- background to the study;
- research subjects;
- research methodology and techniques to be used;
- budget.

A more thorough research proposal will be required on acceptance to the course. This usually needs to be submitted within a few months of enrolment.

Timing your research

You will be required to draw up a timeline for your research. Be realistic about the stages involved: for instance, data-gathering and analysis are a major part of the process. Ask a lecturer to check and make suggestions before you submit your final timeline. The following are stages to include in your timeline:

- literature review;
- full research proposal;
- data collection;
- data analysis;
- drafting of project;
- final writing-up of project.

Gathering data for your research

Plan how you will collect your data and what data are needed to answer your research question. While focusing on the topic, check that you can access the data you need. Your research may require that you use some confidential information, or use services that do not necessarily allow you access. Consult your supervisor about the best methods for gaining permission to access certain data. Sometimes a little effort pays off.

This stage of your research will be guided by your supervisor. It requires a substantial amount of time, so do not underestimate it in your planning. As a researcher, you need to organise the data-gathering process carefully so that you get *all* the information you need at the times you have available to you: for instance, if you have the opportunity to interview patients once only, you must ensure that your interview questions and your equipment are ready. Also, any letters of permission required from ethical bodies should be acquired well in advance and, on the day, be ready in a folder in case you are asked to present them.

Interpreting the data

Do the data answer your research question? This may seem like a strange question, however it has been known for researchers to gather lots of interesting data but not the sort of data that are pertinent to the research question. The *purpose* of the research must remain the *focus* of the research. You need to explain how the data answer your question and point out significant and interesting aspects. If you get more data than you need, it takes too much time to go through it afterwards. The data will be easier to interpret if you are very clear about what you need to collect and focus on.

Writing the chapters

When you are ready for the final writing stage, setting a few rules for yourself can keep you focused and your motivation levels high.

Plan the project. Have a time schedule prepared for each section, with enough time at the end for proofing. This will also ensure that you do not rush any of the stages and have time to accommodate any of the annoying, small things that may go wrong, such as a computer 'crash'. Write something every day. Some researchers have a word limit of 1000 daily to help them maintain a focus even on low-motivation days.

Plan each section. As with any other piece of academic writing, you need to plan carefully. Under each section, note down the headings and subheadings and keep this as a guide. You will probably change the order and wording as part of the drafting process but it will serve its purpose as a clear outline for the writing-up process.

Get into a work rhythm. This may mean starting work at the

same time and place each day, so you can work uninterruptedly for a few hours. It is important not to be distracted and not to leave the writing at difficult points. If you have a work rhythm it is easier to maintain good habits.

You will probably start drafting sections of the research paper as you go along. However, once you have the data collected and analysed you will be in a good position to start the final writing process. Having all the information—that is, the literature, data and analysis—means that you are able to get an overall sense of the argument and make the necessary links between sections.

Drafting is an essential component of the final stage of writing (as described in chapter 6). Work through each section at a time to ensure that all the links are made, ideas are clear, each paragraph has a topic sentence, ideas are in the correct order, and anything that is irrelevant is deleted.

The drafting process involves a careful review of the content of the writing, to ensure that the logic is clear to anyone reading the document. A good way to do this is to imagine that the person reading it has no background in the discipline. This will help you pinpoint areas that may need explanation or clarification.

Logic and clarity are essential elements and should run throughout the thesis. When revising the project as a whole, *cross-referencing* (indicating the links between one point in the text and another) can help you guide readers to points already stated and remind them of interesting aspects that have come up in the argument.

Having time to revise and proofread is essential. The proofing process is more effective when you have been able to put the project down for a week and return to it with a new perspective or 'critical eye'.

Your literature search

During this stage, you will spend a lot of time using the library facilities. Find out about what the library offers in terms of services and material. The sorts of material you will be accessing are journals, books, government reports, theses, abstracts and online texts.

As part of the search, you will gather information you need to help develop your argument. Think about your topic carefully:

• What are the key words you will enter for the search?
• Are you interested only in recent works? How far back do you intend to go?
• Are you interested only in Australian material? What other material may be of interest?
• What type of material may be of assistance—books, journals, theses?
• Who are the specialists in the area?

Once you have located useful material, look at the bibliographies that list the references the authors have used to sift out any further good sources. Like a detective, you will be in a position of following one lead after another until you track down all the information you require.

Researching using the Internet

As information on the Net is not necessarily checked for accuracy or quality, it is your responsibility to critically review the material. You must evaluate the validity and reliability of the information found on the Net before you use it for your studies. Sometimes checking the author, the organisation and whether there are other links to reliable resources will help you analyse the validity of the material. Read the material carefully to see whether it ties in with the other literature.

Recording your sources

Once you have found the information, keep a careful record. Some people like to use index cards, others computer-based bibliographical systems. Whichever you use, make sure it is an easy system. Writing down bibliographical details on bits of paper means you risk losing them and having to search for them again. Instead, keep a good recording system that carefully follows the referencing conventions of the system you are required to use. (Chapter 8 has set out details that will serve as a guide, while chapter 4 explains the use of index cards or the resources record sheet.)

The literature review

At the beginning of this book, the idea of academic discourse is introduced. The literature review is one way to enter the ever-evolving communication in your discipline. It is not just a list of research. Reviewing the literature involves a critical reading of contemporary and important works relating to your topic. As you read, you will take notes of other works that support or oppose your arguments and that relate to your findings. This component of your research project will continue throughout the research period. It demonstrates that you are aware of the arguments in your area of study: it shows that you are taking part in academic discourse. Making links between facts is an important part of the review process. You need to investigate the literature and explain how it fits with the questions you raise in your research.

Methodology

The method of a research project depends on your field of study. Your supervisor will help you identify an appropriate method. In the sciences you may undertake a *laboratory experiment*. Other fields may require a *case study* approach or a *field study* approach.

Surveys are also common tools for research. Ask your lecturer to recommend appropriate texts that will assist you in designing your research method. In the methodology section you need to rationalise:

- your choice of sample group;
- how you will gather the data and why the method you choose is an appropriate one;
- how you will handle or extract meaningful information from the data.

When writing up this section, it helps to have clearly defined subtitles. Under each you can place the features of academic arguments that are of interest—that is, categorise each idea presented under its own heading. This way the reader can easily see the main points of the research study as you have presented them.

Presentation of the project

Departments, faculties and educational institutions often state their own requirements for the presentation of projects. It is important to keep these in mind while you are writing up the project. In particular, you may find it helpful to check on exact details of:

- size of margins;
- presentation of appendixes;
- presentation of figures/tables etc.;
- binding of the thesis/research project;
- length of research (number of words);
- required number of copies;
- to whom the copies are submitted;
- forms to complete with your final submission.

EXAMINATION OF A THESIS

The examination of an honours, master's or PhD-level thesis is usually undertaken by two examiners (not your supervisor), one or both of whom are usually *external* supervisors (from outside the university) with some expertise in your area. It may take eight weeks before you get the examiner's reports and results, so you need to be patient.

The examination of a PhD thesis may require an oral exam or *viva voce*, depending on the university. During this exam, you will be asked questions about your research findings, methodology, interpretation of the data, reading and so on. The main aim is to demonstrate to the examiners that you have a good understanding of your research topic.

Once your thesis has been accepted, you will be notified and given instructions as to its preparation for binding and submission. One copy of the thesis is placed in the library, where it can be accessed by other interested people.

COPING WITH SOLITUDE

As research studies require a lot of self-directed study, contact with staff and other students can fall off when you are not attending classes, and being away from home and family can add to the feeling of solitude. This is why it is important to keep a balanced program of sport or other activities, work (if relevant) and study. Forcing yourself to sit all day, every day and do research can take away your inspiration and motivation, which will not assist you in doing your best work. Give yourself a little reward for the work you do: for instance, if you write a chapter according to your study plan, take a day off for an excursion. Another way of treating yourself is to join the postgraduate association at university, which holds social events (as well as academic workshops). It may be a good way to meet others who are doing research and share experiences in a social situation.

SECTIONS OF A RESEARCH PROJECT

Generally, a research study contains set sections (see box on the next page). It is best to check with your supervisor for any subject-specific conventions that may be required.

SECTIONS OF A RESEARCH PROJECT

Title page
Dedication (if any)/acknowledgments
Declaration
Table of contents
Abstract
List of tables (if any)
List of figures (if any)
Introduction
Chapters
• Literature review
• Research question
• Subjects
• Methodology
• Results
• Discussion
• Recommendations
Conclusion
Appendixes
Bibliography

Title page

This includes your research title, your name, date submitted, institution, your supervisor's name and the degree for which the thesis is presented. Try to make the title short and interesting.

Dedication

This is an optional page on which you may dedicate the study to someone, such as a family member or spouse. Under the heading 'Acknowledgments' you may include a list of people you would like to mention for their involvement or support.

Declaration

This involves writing a short statement declaring that the thesis or research project has not been submitted as part of degree studies previously and that all acknowledgments to references have been made.

Table of contents

The table of contents lists the sections and subsections and their page numbers in the study. It provides a sequential overview of the document, which assists the reader in locating different sections. The box below gives an example of how to set out this table using roman and arabic numerals.

Abstract

This is a brief statement at the beginning of the project that clearly summarises the research topic, the methodology used and the results found. This lets anyone who is reading the study, such as your examiners, know what to expect when reading the study.

List of figures/list of tables

Any figures or tables used can be indicated just as in a report.

Introduction

As in any introduction, this section gives the reader a clear idea of the issue that will be presented in the study and the general context of the research problem. It also outlines the general organisation of the study. This section is important as it needs to capture the reader's interest.

Literature review

This section allows you to examine and present what is already known about aspects relating to your research topic: developments, breakthroughs, innovative approaches or ideas, controversial theories and so on. It demonstrates that you know the background to your research topic.

Research question

In this section you need to define what you are researching and why. The research question must be stated succinctly and clearly so that the reader is not confused.

Subjects

This section outlines the essential background of the subjects used in the study. For instance, if you are looking at differences in female and male participation in language studies, important details would include the number of subjects of each gender, the age groups, perhaps whether the language students are from one school or many, whether public or private schools and so on.

Methodology

The method for data-gathering and analysis are defined and justified in this section. The relevance of the data is discussed in terms of choosing an appropriate research analysis tool and the reliability of your data needs to be presented. Read other successful research studies to get an idea of how this section functions. These documents are usually kept in the library.

Results

Important statistics or results are presented and explained here. This part of the document gives you the opportunity to present the results that relate specifically to your arguments.

Discussion

This is the researcher's opportunity to discuss the importance of the work done and how it contributes to the body of work that already exists, thus linking issues back to the literature review. If there are contradictions, differences or similarities you should say why these may have occurred.

Recommendations

This section, although at first it may seem odd, provides a useful discussion of general research directions that may be followed, based on your research, the existing research and the limitations of your research. This will not demonstrate flaws, but will demonstrate that you have thought about the study and are able to perceive areas that need further research or improvement.

Conclusion

Here, you draw together the important points raised in the study. You, as researcher, can state how the general research on the topic and theories have changed as a result of your study, explaining the contribution that your study has made to the discipline.

Appendixes

This section contains any information or results that are relevant to the study but which do not fit into the main part of it (because they interrupt the flow of information).

Bibliography

A detailed list of all the articles, books and other material used in undertaking the research should be included as the last section.

CONCLUSION

Postgraduate-level study does require more work and a stronger sense of commitment than undergraduate study; however, with careful choice of courses, planning and preparation, the rewards will make it all worthwhile. The strategies and information presented here have been found to be useful by students new to postgraduate-level studies. These ideas, along with your own study strategies and lecturer assistance, should give you a valuable study experience.

✓ CHECKLIST FOR RESEARCH STUDY

☐ Become familiar with library resources.

☐ Have a set schedule of appointments with your supervisor.

☐ Have a time management plan that is realistic.

☐ Check on assistance with gathering and analysing data.

☐ Ask about assistance with language issues.

☐ Ask about useful short courses, such as research planning, thesis writing.

☐ Attend all classes.

☐ Keep a good resources record system.

☐ Keep a back-up of all work done on computer.

☐ Reward yourself for achievements.

14

Using technology

Throughout this book you will have come across references to using different types of technological equipment that are, by now, standard tools in tertiary study—CD-ROMs, computerised library catalogues, the Internet and so on. While some students are familiar with the use of some of the technology found in a tertiary institution, others will never have come across the equipment or never have been required to use it before.

Courses are held to help students learn to use technological resources. Information about these courses is usually made available through daily newsletters, newspapers, notices on pinboards and through staff. Check with the student union for the particular training courses you are interested in. Normally, these are run at the beginning of semester, so do not delay getting your name registered.

WORD PROCESSORS

A commonly used tool is the word processor. It allows you to type in a document, change it numerous times, do a spellcheck, present it professionally and print copies. You do not even have to know how to type to use it, though it does help to practise and build up a recognition of where the keys are.

Presentation of assignments

The key to presenting assignments professionally is simplicity and consistency. Formats for different written assignments have already been explained in earlier chapters but a few helpful presentation tips are outlined here.

- Both left and right *margins* should be at least 3 centimetres in width.
- Each *heading* should stand out clearly. The main heading should be differentiated from subheadings or section headings: this can be done by using bold or underlining. The same style or font and size of letters should be used for all sub- or section headings. This also applies to any tables, figures or charts that are included.
- The same *style* of writing should be used throughout the text.
- Each *paragraph* should be separated by one blank line. No indentations are necessary.
- *Footnotes* and *endnotes* are simplified by the facility on the word processor that inserts and numbers them automatically. It even changes the order automatically if you add or delete a note.
- *Tables* can be constructed easily once you have practised using this facility. It allows you to design a table of different-sized columns and rows.
- *Number each page* either at the top right-hand corner or the bottom of the page.
- *Print preview* allows you to look at how your page will look and to make any changes before you print out your final copy.
- Do not forget to include an attractive *title page*, with all the necessary details outlined. Start off making a good impression.

- *Spellcheck* each document before you print it out, then check for spelling errors by proofreading. Do not submit an assignment with careless spelling errors.
- *Saving your document* is essential. Having a working disk and a back-up disk is a good way to ensure that if one disk is ruined you have another copy handy. Save your documents often while working, just in case someone pulls the plug accidentally; then you will not have lost hours' worth of work.
- *Keep a copy* of your work for yourself. The assignment might get lost and you would then be in the position of having to redo it.
- *Virus-check* the computer before you use it, particularly when it is used by others. There is nothing worse than working hard on a document to find it cannot be saved or printed out because of a virus.

Grammar check

A grammar check looks at every sentence and ascertains whether there is a subject, verb and object order, whether it is too long and complicated, whether plurals and singulars agree and so on. However, language is more complicated and elaborate than a grammar check allows and each writer has his/her own style. Be wary of using grammar checks unless you have an excellent grasp of English grammar rules and can make appropriate choices— otherwise it may end up being a long, confusing and useless exercise.

Spreadsheets

Computer spreadsheets mean that a lot of numerical or word-based information can be recorded, added, deleted and generally managed easily. Spreadsheets can be printed out to provide a comprehensive and clearly presented list of information.

Statistical analyses

There are a number of different statistical packages available that allow you to type in a lot of data. The packages run parametric or non-parametric tests and come up with areas of significance or non-significance relating to an area of research. Your lecturers will guide you in your choice and use of such packages.

THE INTERNET

The Internet or Net has caused a lot of excitement at universities because it allows the user to access a vast amount of information throughout the world via the World Wide Web (WWW or Web). By clicking on words and images, users can trace information on a topic without any constraints on distance and time (the Net is open at all hours, unlike a library). In fact, the amount of information can be daunting and hours can go by sifting through it all.

There are a few problems with using the Web that should be considered. A lot of the information that is put on the Web can be defined as publicity, trivia, misleading or biased. Organisations use the Web increasingly to publicise services or products. Sometimes the publicity is presented as research-style information, so a user needs to be aware of the source to make an informed decision about the objectivity and subsequent value of the information. Some of the material is just a load of rubbish which is not useful to studies and can be frustrating when you have spent a long time waiting for the information to come up on your screen.

Anyone can publish on the Web: there are no editors or publishing experts to check the information for inaccuracy or bias. It is essential that students using the information on the Web examine the material presented critically. Critical thinking about information and its validity is an important part of the research process.

Another drawback of using the Web is that it can be time-consuming—following one link after another only to find that you have been *dumped*; that the link no longer exists or the Net, for some reason, will not operate. You find yourself at the end of a long search having to start all over again. One way of avoiding this is to bookmark interesting sites, so that if you are dumped you can click on the bookmark and return to the exact site quickly. Bookmarks can always be deleted later. Also, you can make notes about the links in your notebook (the Web address and a brief explanation on the material) to help you find the site again.

Searching the Web

To find information on the Web, you can either type the address which identifies the site or you can do a general search using a search engine (e.g. Yahoo! or AltaVista). An Internet address is called a Uniform Resources Locator (or URL). The address provides you with information as to its source (see Figure 14.1). Other common organisational abbreviations used in Australia are: edu, educational; gov, government; net, network resources; org, organisation; and com, commercial.

Figure 14.2 shows what you would see if you looked up the Web page for Allen & Unwin. The address is typed in the line

Figure 14.1   Sample URL

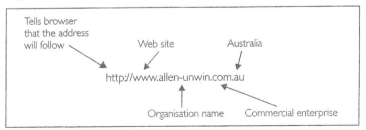

Figure 14.2 Sample Web page

at the top and the homepage comes up. The homepage is like a title page, which usually lists the contents of that site.

Some basic commands

To go back to a previous page, all you have to do is click on Back, or you can go forward to a page by clicking on Forward. If a search is taking too long or you have changed your mind, you can click on Stop. The search will stop and wait for your next instructions. If you would like to print out a document click on Print. Remember to note down the date on the printout for referencing purposes (see chapter 8).

Doing a general search on the Web

If you wanted information on a topic but did not have any addresses, you could use a *search engine* to locate this information.

Search engines are huge indexes of Web sites and will provide you with many links. Some of the more popular search engine addresses are listed in the box below. However, think about what you are going to type when you are asked for key words. A key word such as 'marketing' will produce thousands of links, a lot of them useless. Narrowing your topic to 'marketing theories Australia' might be more valid when starting a general search, although this might overlook 'marketing theory'. In this case you might use the asterisk (*) to include both words: thus, typing 'marketing theor* Australia' would have the advantage of calling up relevant information under both titles. Also, be aware that some search engines will look for each word and list everything found for each word. To have the search engine read the whole line and list appropriate sites, add the symbol '+' between each word (e.g. marketing + theor* + Australia).

Useful search engines	
AltaVista	http://altavista.digital.com
Yahoo!	http://www.yahoo.com
Lycos	http://www.lycos.com
Open Text	http://www.opentext.com
Web Crawler	http://webcrawler.com
Infoseek	http://www.infoseek.com

ELECTRONIC MAIL (E-MAIL)

E-mail is now used widely as a means of communicating quickly with people. Your lecturers will have e-mail, and may invite you to communicate with them in this way if you have any questions. You compose your message just as you would write a letter, although e-mail messages tend to be less formal than letters, as you will find out when you gain experience in using it.

Your institution will allocate a user name and password to each student. These details should remain confidential, and will

Figure 14.3 Sample e-mail message

To:	LW@rocketmail.com.au
From:	Teresa.defazio@vu.edu.au
Re:	Project

Hello Luca!

Thank you for sending me the project so quickly. I have had a look at it and it looks fine. The references need a bit of work as there are some inconsistencies in the bibliography. Don't forget the Harvard system is the one used in this faculty. I have added a few comments, but overall it looks like you have done some excellent planning and drafting. Well done! Feel free to drop in when it suits you to pick it up.

Regards

give you access to a computer. The institution may set up an e-mail address for you, which anyone can use who wants to send you a message. Teresa.defazio@vu.edu.au is my e-mail address. It includes my name, the organisation for which I work, 'edu' demonstrates that it is an educational institution, while 'au' demonstrates that the organisation is situated in Australia.

Each computer will have a particular e-mail service and you will be given instructions on how to access that service. Sending and receiving messages is a similar process. You type in the e-mail address of the person with whom you will be corresponding in the space provided, add your e-mail details and a few words indicating what the message is about. The computer will automatically add the time and date. Below you will see a bigger space where you can add the message. Once you have finished composing your message, click on $\boxed{\text{Send}}$ and the message will go to the address you have typed in. Figure 14.3 is an example.

To check whether you have received mail, click on $\boxed{\text{Mail}}$. Sometimes this is indicated by an envelope symbol. This will list all the mail you have received. Select the message you want to read; once you have read it, you can print it, save it or delete it.

OTHER RESOURCES

Preparing presentation slides

There are a number of useful packages that can be used to prepare attractive overheads, cover pages and illustrations. One of the most popular packages used in oral presentations is Powerpoint, which allows you to organise text and images in a way that helps make an impact. Clip art packages are common, as these allow you to organise pictures and some text, though the text facility is limited compared with Powerpoint. Check to see whether there are any training courses in the use of these at your institution.

Computer-aided design programs

Computer-aided design (CAD) programs are increasingly being used in such disciplines as architecture, art and engineering. Techniques on how to use the programs will be covered in your studies.

Student computer laboratories

Most institutions have several computer laboratories for students. Some are in faculties and are equipped with specialist programs needed for courses, others are for general student use and can be accessed on presentation of your student card. Normally, computer laboratories can also be accessed on weekends, weeknights and semester breaks.

CONCLUSION

It is natural to get nervous about using the various technological resources you will encounter during your studies. Nonetheless, there are courses you can undertake to get the necessary information. After a little practice you will gain the confidence to adopt these tools as part of your study equipment.

Appendixes

I. AUSTRALIAN IDIOMS

ace! beauty!	excellent, great
aggro (noun)	aggression, violence
clear the air	eliminate tension from a situation
up in the air	not resolved, undecided
Akubra	Australian-style broad-brimmed cowboy hat
amber fluid	beer
she's right	everything is OK
arvo	afternoon
Aussie Rules	Australian Rules Football
bad egg	a nasty person
barbie	barbecue
bash	party
bloke	fellow, man
bonkers	crazy
booze	alcoholic drink
BYO	bring your own
cocky	arrogant, conceited

smart cookie	smart person
cop	policeman
cossie/cozzie	swimsuit
dillydally	waste time, procrastinate
dirt cheap	inexpensive
dole	unemployment benefits
to go Dutch	each person pays his/her own expenses
fair dinkum	true, honest, genuine
flake out	collapse because of exhaustion
freebie	something given free of charge
galah	fool, stupid person
gawk	stare foolishly
get-together	informal party or gathering
grog	alcohol
grub	food
grotty	dirty
on the house	free, a gift
I'm joshing	I'm joking
Kiwi	New Zealander
get some kip	have a nap
mate	friend
have/get some nosh	have a snack or food
posh	elegant, smart, luxurious
right as rain	everything is fine/OK
shout	pay for something for a person
smoko	tea break at work
smooth sailing	easy
stubby	small bottle of beer
keep on track	stay focused, work to reach an objective
bangers	sausages
wag school	deliberately stay away from school
wally	stupid person, fool
hard yakka	work (usually manual)

2. COMMON NOTE-TAKING ABBREVIATIONS

i.e.	that is
→	leads to
@	at
+	and
e.g.	example
≈	approximately
n	number
min	minimum
max	maximum
sub	subject
bk	book
info	information
gov	government
u/s	understand(ing)
>	greater than
<	less than
w	with
w/o	without
b/c	because
∴	therefore

3. RESOURCES RECORD SHEET

Author surname	Author initials	Date published	Title	Publisher	Place	Pages	Type of document (dated and cited if applicable)	Call no.	Comments on content (Web address if applicable)

4. COMMONLY USED INSTRUCTION WORDS

analyse/examine   break the subject into components and write about how these parts relate to each other—whether there are any tensions. You need to look at *how* and *why*

discuss/comment   note down the interesting aspects relating to a topic and why these are of interest to people in your field of study. Try not to bring too many points into your essay. Include your point of view on these aspects and supporting evidence. Focus on major aspects, particularly if you have a small word limit

describe/explain   talk about the facts or an event or a process. You do not need to interpret these—just point out main issues or aspects

outline   present the main points of an issue in an ordered or sequential way

contrast/compare   present similarities and differences between two issues, events, procedures, phenomena, works and so on. Identify some aspects of, for instance, two works of literature, and see how each of these aspects is dealt with in each work. Do not try to write about too many aspects: dealing with two or three thoroughly is better than dealing with five or six superficially

evaluate   consider a text, a theory, an approach, a situation, and make your own judgment of its strengths and weaknesses

review   examine, analyse and interpret the
                              main issues relating to a topic

summarise   present just the main ideas of a text,
                              argument, idea, approach or procedure.
                              Do not include details

5. PUNCTUATION MARKS

(	)	brackets or parentheses
'	'	quotation marks or inverted commas
. . .		ellipsis
.		full stop or period
,		comma
;		semicolon
:		colon
*		asterisk
-		hyphen
'		apostrophe
[	]	square brackets
/		slash
?		question mark
!		exclamation mark

6. CONNECTIVES OR CONJUNCTIONS

Joining ideas
first
second
third
finally
also
in additon to
additionally
moreover
furhter
furthermore
again

Expressing time
prior to
before
after
afterwards
meanwhile
then

Similar points of view
equally
likewise
similarly
accordingly
in addition

Expressing results
thus
therefore
so
consequently
hence
as a result

Explaining
for example
for instance
that is
in other words
in particular

Clarifying
in other words
to reiterate
in essence
briefly

Expressing importance
above all
significantly
an important
more importantly

Concluding
to sum up
in summary
in short
to conclude

in fact

in conclusion

importantly

in brief

in other words

Expressing different points of view

in contrast	however	although	in spite of
in comparison	but	nevertheless	besides
on the contrary	yet	nonetheless	alternatively
on the other hand	though	despite	or

7. CRITERIA FOR PRESENTATIONS

Topic _____

	Excellent	Very Good	Good	Pass	Poor
Structure					
• Focused on topic					
• Logical structure					
• Presented as a team (if applicable)					
• Moved from one main point to another smoothly					
Content					
• Introduction clear					
• Main ideas clear					
• Conclusion clear					
• Important points covered					
• Relevant material					
• Relevant support material					
• Used no repetition					
Style					
• Confident presentation					
• Appropriate speaking pace (not too fast or too slow)					
• No reading from notes					
• Easy to hear					
• Eye contact					
Visual Aids					
• Easily followed					
• Not crowded with information					
• Relevant to presentation					
Overall					
• Well prepared					
• Clearly presented					
• Easy to follow					

8. WEEKLY TIMETABLE

Time	Monday	Tuesday	Wednesday	Thursday	Friday	Saturday	Sunday
9.00–10.00							
10.00–11.00							
11.00–12.00							
12.00–1.00							
1.00–2.00							
2.00–3.00							
3.00–4.00							
4.00–5.00							
5.00–6.00							
6.00–7.00							
7.00–8.00							
8.00–9.00							
9.00–10.00							

9. SEMESTER STUDY SCHEDULE

Week	Subject:	Subject:	Subject:	Subject:	Subject:	Subject:
1						
2						
3						
4						
5						
6						
7						
8						
9						
10						
11						
12						
13						

Glossary

abstract	a summary of the main points presented in the essay/report/thesis etc.
appendix	a section at the end of a document which contains additional information to that presented in the body of the text (e.g. chart, table, graph, questionnaire)
bibliography	a list of resources referred to by the author in the text
blurb	information about the book, usually found on the back cover
bookmark	something used to mark a place in a book, or (Net) to save a Web site on the computer
brainstorming	spontaneous discussion and forming of ideas
browser	a program that reads documents (e.g. Netscape, Lynx, Internet Explorer) on the Internet. It selects documents and goes from one document to another

catalogue	a list of authors, titles etc. arranged in order for referencing purposes. Library catalogues are mainly computerised
CD-ROM	(Compact Disc Read Only Memory); looks like an audio disk and may contain visual, text and audio information
chronologically	arranging of events according to date, time or alphabetical order
cliché	an overused phrase
conjunctions	*see* connectives
connectives	words and phrases used to link ideas and help the flow of an argument
copyright	a law which stipulates that only a certain amount of a text may be copied as a single copy for individual use. Does not allow copying without parts of a texts being acknowledged, or making multiple copies without first obtaining special permission from the publisher
cross-referencing	indicates the links between one point in the text and another
data	facts or information
discipline	area of study. Recognised disciplines include business, science, engineering
dissertation	*see* thesis
dumped (getting)	(Net) losing one's place when using computer because of a user or computer error
ELICOS	English Language Intensive Courses for Overseas Students
e-mail	abbreviation for electronic mail. This program allows you to receive messages and send messages using e-mail addresses

FAQ — acronym, or abbreviation for 'frequently asked questions'. Usually it is part of a Web site, and contains information that users ask about regularly

field of studies — area of study, or discipline

font — style of type on the word processor

FTP — acronym, or abbreviation for file transfer protocol. Allows you to upload files on the Internet or download files from your computer to, for instance, your disk

homepage — the welcome or title page of a Web site. Usually includes an index of other pages linked to the site

homestay — an organisation that arranges accommodation for international students with families in Australia

hyperlink — a link that allows you to jump to another link on the Net. For example, you can click on a word or picture and link up to another site on the Web. Links are usually in a different colour and/or underlined so they stand out from the text; also, the cursor changes to a hand symbol when it is over a link

hypertext — a piece of text (e.g. a word or phrase that allows you to link up with another written document or site on the Internet)

Internet — or Net: a world-wide collection of joined networks of computers. E-mail and the World Wide Web are part of the Internet

jargon — words or phrases familiar only to a profession or group

journals	a periodical publication that presents information on a particular discipline
login	(noun): your account name that allows you to access a computer system. Usually you will see the prompts Login and Password
modem	a hardware that connects your computer and phone line to link the computer to other computers
OHTs	acronym for overhead transparencies
online	using (being on) the Internet (WWW)
paragraphs	units of writing that present a main idea followed by supporting details
paraphrase	expressing meaning using other words (e.g. in a summary)
password	a code used to access a secure system: for instance, you may have a password to enter e-mail so that it can be viewed only by you
periodicals	*see* journals
plagiarism	using another person's words or ideas and presenting them as one's own
postgraduate	(course or student) studies that follow undergraduate courses
proofing	involves checking writing for typing errors, spelling, reference omissions and presentation aspects
quoting	citing or copying something from a text
reference	information such as author and publishing details that relate to a citation
referencing system	a particular style that dictates how reference details should be set out
search engine	similar to a catalogue system. It searches for a topic/name etc. AltaVista and Yahoo! are examples

synopsis	a brief summary of the essay/report/ presentation
tertiary education	the third level of education after primary and secondary school
thesaurus	a sort of dictionary that lists concepts or words according to their meaning
thesis	a lengthy research paper, usually written as part of postgraduate-level study
thesis statement	a statement that outlines the main idea
topic sentence	states the main idea of a paragraph
transcript	a record of an individual student study progress
undergraduate	(course or student) bachelor degree or first-level studies at university
URL	acronym, or abbreviation for 'Uniform Resources Locator'. Simply, it acts as an Internet address
WWW	acronym for World Wide Web. The Web is a collection of many resources that are all linked together—like a library of information that you can access

Useful references

Writing

Bate, D. & Sharpe, S. 1996, *Writer's Handbook: For University Students*, Harcourt Brace, Sydney.

Germov, J. 1996, *Get Great Marks for Your Essays*, Allen & Unwin, Sydney.

Osland, D., Boyd, D., McKenna, W. & Salusinszky, I. 1991, *Writing in Australia: A Composition Course for Tertiary Students*, Harcourt Brace Jovanovich Group, Sydney.

Research projects

Anderson, J. & Poole, M. 1994, *Thesis and Assignment Writing*, 3rd edn, Jacaranda Wiley, Brisbane.

Bell, J. 1987, *Doing Your Research Project: A Guide for First-Time Researchers in Education and Social Science*, Open University Press, Milton Keynes.

Day, R. 1995, *How to Write and Publish a Scientific Paper*, 4th edn, Cambridge University Press, Cambridge.

Elphinstone, L. & Schweitzer, R. 1998, *How to Get a Research Degree*, Allen & Unwin, Sydney.

Evans, D. 1995, *How to Write a Better Thesis or Report*, Melbourne University Press, Melbourne.

Phillips, E.M. & Pugh, D.S. 1994, *How to Get a PhD: A Handbook for Students and Their Supervisors, 2nd edn*, Open University Press, Milton Keynes.

Science

Rhoden, C. & Starkey, R. 1998, *Studying Science at University: Everything you Need to Know*, Allen & Unwin, Sydney.

Silyn-Roberts, H. 1996, *Writing for Science: A Practical Handbook for Social Science, Engineering & Technology Students*, Addison-Wesley Longman, Auckland.

Business law

Crosling, G.M. & Murphy, H. 1994, *How to Study Business Law: Reading, Writing and Exams*, Butterworths, Sydney.

Social sciences

Betts, K. & Seitz, A. 1994, *Writing Essays and Research Reports in the Social Sciences, 2nd edn*, Nelson, Melbourne.

Accounting

Cotesta, P.V., Crosling, G.M. & Murphy, H. 1998, *Writing for Accounting Students*, Butterworths, Sydney.

Psychology

O'Shea, R.P. 1996, *Writing for Psychology, 2nd edn*, Harcourt Brace, Sydney.

Medicine

Hutton, A.R. 1993, *An Introduction to Medical Terminology: A Self-Teaching Package*, Churchill Livingstone, Edinburgh.

Referencing

Li, X. & Crane, N. 1993, *Electronic Style: A Guide to Citing Information*, Meckler, Westport, CT.

MLA Handbook for Writers of Research Papers, 1995, 4th edn, J. Gibaldi (ed.), MLA, New York.

Publication Manual of the American Psychological Association, 1983, 3rd edn, APA, Washington.

Style Manual for Authors, Editors and Printers, 1988, 5th edn, Australian Government Publishing Service, Canberra.

Web site guide for citing Net resources: http://www.library. wisc.edu./libraries/Memorial/citing.htm

Guide for international students

Ballard, B. & Clanchy, J. 1984, *Study Abroad: A Manual for Asian Students*, Longman, Malaysia.

Australian idioms

Howard, P. 1997, *Oz Slang*, Jim Coroneos, Sydney.

Macquaire University 1984, *Aussie Talk: The Macquaire Dictionary of Australian Colloquialisms*, Macquarie Library, Sydney.

Dictionary and thesauruses

Candlin, C.N. & Blair, D. (eds). 1997, *The Australian Learner's Dictionary*, NCELTR, Sydney.

Bernard, J.R.L. (ed.) 1986, *The Macquarie Thesaurus*, Macquarie Library, Sydney.

Roget, P.M. 1984, *Roget's Thesaurus of English Words and Phrases*, Penguin, Harmondsworth.

Interesting Web sites

Australian Broadcasting Council (ABC) — http://www.abc.com.au

Australian Copyright Council Web sites — http://www.copyright.org.au
http://www.gradschools.com
http://www.studyboard.com

Australian Government Publishing Service — http://www.agps.gov.au

Council of Australian Postgraduate Associations (CAPA) — http://www.ozemail.com.au/
~postgrad
http://capa.edu.au

National Postgraduate Research Database — http://www.scu.edu.au/
sponsored/ngrdb/

Newspapers

The Age — http://www.theage.com.au

The Australian — http://www.theaustralian.com.au

The Australian Financial Review — http://www.afr.com.au

A link to Australian and international newspapers — http://www.nla.gov.au/oz/
npapers.htm

The Sydney Morning Herald — http://www.smh.com.au

Electronic journals

Site to access some electronic journals — http://www.nla.gov.au/oz/
ausejour

Universities

College and university homepages — http:///www.genesis.net.au/
links/unis/cdemello

Information on TAFE studies

http://www.otfe.vic.giv.au/studinfo

Australian libraries   http://www.nla.gov.au/libraries/

Site of interest for international students
Australian International   http://www.aief.edu.au/
   Education Foundation   studguide/studying.htm

Index